W9-CIG-442

WITHDRAWN

F. R. Leavis

Twayne's English Authors Series

Kinley Roby, Editor

TEAS 560

F. R. LEAVIS
CORBIS/Hulton-Deutsch Collection

F. R. Leavis

John Ferns

McMaster University

Twayne Publishers
New York

Twayne's English Authors Series No. 560

F. R. Leavis
John Ferns

Copyright © 2000 by Twayne Publishers

Twayne Publishers
1633 Broadway
New York, NY 10019

Library of Congress Cataloging-in-Publication Data
Ferns, John, 1941–
    F.R. Leavis / John Ferns.
        p. cm. — (Twayne's English authors series ; TEAS 560)
    Includes bibliographical references and index.
    ISBN 0-8057-1615-7 (alk. paper)
        1. Leavis, F. R. (Frank Raymond), 1895-2. English literature—History and criticism—Theory, etc. 3. Literature—History and criticism—Theory, etc. 4. Criticism—England—History—20th century. I. Title. II. Series.

PR55.L43 F47 2000
801'.95'092—dc21   99-087421

This paper meets the requirements of ANSI/NISO Z3948-1992 (Permanence of Paper).

10 9 8 7 6 5 4 3 2 1

Printed in the United States of America

To Gillian and Maureen Ferns

Contents

Preface

Frank Raymond Leavis (1895–1978) is arguably the greatest English literary critic of the twentieth century, the natural successor to Samuel Johnson and Matthew Arnold. Important, from the beginning, in championing the work of T. S. Eliot and D. H. Lawrence, he developed from the Cambridge English of his undergraduate days a critical method that, growing out of close analysis of literary texts, sought to evaluate the cultural significance of works of literature. Judgment was crucial to Leavis, and his standards were high. He was interested in discussing only major writers whose works he considered to be of sufficient quality.

The present, seven chapter study begins with an account of Leavis's life and career as a critic. Particular attention is paid to the impact of World War I upon the idealistic, young history student who enlisted in the Friends' Ambulance Unit in 1915 at the end of his first year of university. Leavis's response to the war is likened to Wordsworth's response to the French Revolution—cataclysmic events that permanently affected both. The second chapter considers Leavis's early career as a critic following his completion of undergraduate studies. He changed from History to English on his return to Cambridge University in 1919. In the chapter, I discuss Leavis's doctoral thesis, "The Relationship of Journalism to Literature: Studied in the Rise and Earlier Development of the Press in England," completed under the supervision of Sir Arthur Quiller-Couch, as well as his early pamphlets *Mass Civilisation and Minority Culture* (1930) and *D. H. Lawrence* (1930) published by Leavis's student Gordon Fraser's Minority Press. The chapter concludes with a consideration of Leavis's first major publication, *New Bearings in English Poetry: A Study of the Contemporary Situation* (1932), in which he discusses the reorientation he perceived in modern English poetry. Chapter 3 completes discussion of, what I regard as, the first phase of Leavis's critical career with consideration of *Revaluation: Tradition and Development in English Poetry* (1936), in which he presents "new bearings" in the tradition of English poetry from Donne to Keats. Leavis argues that with the "dislodgement" of Milton and his replacement by Donne, whose poetry is related directly to the dramatic verse of Shakespeare, a new view of the canon of English poetry emerges.

In the fourth chapter, I discuss Leavis's criticism of the novel, in particular his idea of the novel as dramatic poem, and his delineation of a great tradition in English fiction that runs from Jane Austen through George Eliot to Henry James and Joseph Conrad. Also, I briefly discuss Leavis's changing response to Dickens, and his perception of an even greater vital tradition in English writing that runs from Shakespeare through Blake to Dickens and D. H. Lawrence. Chapter 5 discusses Leavis's famous reply to C. P. Snow's Rede Lecture "The Two Cultures and the Scientific Revolution" (1959) in his Richmond Lecture of 1962. It proceeds by considering the five further postretirement lectures delivered in the United States and Britain during the 1960s that Leavis gathered in *Nor Shall My Sword: Discourses on Pluralism, Compassion, and Social Hope* (1972).

In the sixth chapter of the study, I discuss Leavis's final assessments, in *The Living Principle: "English" As a Discipline of Thought* (1975) and *Thought, Words, and Creativity: Art and Thought in Lawrence* (1976), of T. S. Eliot and D. H. Lawrence, the writers he regarded, respectively, as the greatest poet and the greatest novelist of the twentieth century. The study concludes with a seventh chapter in which I attempt to estimate Leavis's present importance as a literary and cultural critic.

Acknowledgments

First I must thank Gillian Ferns for her help in the preparation of my manuscript. Without her continuous help the work would not have been completed. Next I must thank McMaster University for granting me research leave for the academic year 1997–1998, during which most of my work was carried out. Also, I would like to thank the following colleagues and friends who have both recently and over many years discussed with and helped me to understand the work of F. R. Leavis: Don Adams, Lionel Adey, Maqbool Aziz, Michael Bell, Brian Crick, Christopher Drummond, Gillian Ferns, the late H. S. Ferns, David Holbrook, W. J. Keith, Brian Lee, Duke Maskell, Pat Menon, Robert Nielsen, Ian Robinson, John Roy, William Shearman, Laurence Steven, Anthony Trott, and Garry Watson.

Permission to quote from the writings of F. R. Leavis has been kindly granted by his literary executors, Dr. L. R. Leavis and Professor G. S. Singh.

Chronology

1895	July 14, Frank Raymond Leavis born at 64 Mill Road, Cambridge, England, to Harry and Kate Sarah Moore Leavis.
1903–1910	After attending Eden Street Infants' School, attends Paradise Street Higher Grade School.
1907	Family moves to 6 Chesterton Hall Crescent.
1910	February 24, awarded "Mr Starr's Prize for English" at City Guildhall. Autumn, attends Cambridge and County School, then the Perse School, Cambridge.
1913	Wins scholarship to Emmanuel College, Cambridge to read for the History Tripos.
1914–1915	Completes first year of university at Emmanuel College.
1915	June, earns satisfactory performance in examinations. Withdraws from university. October, joins Friends' Ambulance Unit at York.
1916	July 8, sails to France. August 16, begins 21 months of work on Ambulance Train Number 5 as cook then nursing orderly.
1919	January 2, demobilized. Spring, takes part one of the History Tripos. Summer, decides to switch to English.
1921	May 22, Father dies, fatally injured in a motorcycle accident, while Leavis is preparing for his final examinations. June, Leavis receives a First Class degree in the English Tripos. Awarded Emmanuel Research Studentship for doctoral studies.
1924	December, receives Ph.D. for thesis on "The Relationship of Journalism to Literature: Studied in the Rise and Earlier Development of the Press in England," supervised by Sir Arthur Quiller-Couch.
1925	January, becomes a college lecturer offering a course on "Literature and Society from the Restoration to the

Death of Johnson." Also undertakes freelance college supervision.

1927   January, offered a probationary faculty lectureship. Gives courses in "Twentieth Century Poetry" and "Critics and Critical Problems." Autumn, meets Queenie Dorothy Roth, a tutee at Girton College.

1929   February, engaged to Queenie Dorothy Roth. September 16, married. Autumn, probationary lectureship contract extended for two years. Mother dies.

1930   *Mass Civilisation and Minority Culture* and *D. H. Lawrence* published by Gordon Fraser's Minority Press.

1931   January, probationary faculty lectureship not renewed. March, moves into family home 6 Chesterton Hall Crescent. Appointed Director of Studies in English at Downing College.

1932   February, *New Bearings in English Poetry* published and April, Q. D. Leavis's doctoral dissertation, *Fiction and the Reading Public,* published, both by Chatto and Windus. May, *Scrutiny: A Quarterly Review* begun. After early issues, Leavis becomes principal editor. *How to Teach Reading: A Primer for Ezra Pound* published by Minority Press.

1933   *For Continuity* published by Minority Press. *Culture and Environment: The Training of Critical Awareness,* with Denys Thompson, published by Chatto and Windus.

1934   January, son Ralph born. *Determinations,* a selection of essays from *Scrutiny,* published by Chatto and Windus.

1936   March, offered college lectureship at Downing. October, appointed probationary university lecturer (part-time) for three years. December, elected fellow of Downing College. *Revaluation: Tradition and Development in English Poetry* published by Chatto and Windus.

1939   September, daughter Kate Laura born. Part-time lectureship extended.

1943   *Education and the University: A Sketch for an "English School"* published by Chatto and Windus.

1944   December, son Lawrence Robin born.

1947   Offered full-time university lectureship.

1948   *The Great Tradition: George Eliot, Henry James, and Joseph Conrad* published by Chatto and Windus.

1951   Family moves to 16 Newton Road, Cambridge.

1952   January, *The Common Pursuit* published by Chatto and Windus.

1953   *Scrutiny: A Quarterly Review* ceases publication.

1955   Autumn, *D. H. Lawrence: Novelist* published by Chatto and Windus.

1959   May, appointed University Reader in English.

1962   February, delivers Richmond Lecture at Downing College, "Two Cultures? The Significance of C. P. Snow." Moves to 12 Bulstrode Gardens, Cambridge. Retires from full-time lecturing and supervision.

1963   October, *Scrutiny* reprinted by Cambridge University Press with a Retrospect by F. R. Leavis.

1964   March, delivers Chichele Lecture at All Souls College, Oxford on *Little Dorrit.* July, resigns Downing College fellowship.

1965   Accepts visiting professorship at University of York and later receives an honorary degree from York. Autumn, F. R. and Q. D. Leavis give lectures and seminars in Finland. Receives honorary degree from University of Leeds.

1966   March, breach with the F. R. Leavis Lectureship Trust. October, F. R. and Q. D. Leavis lecture at Cornell University and Harvard University.

1967   Delivers Clark Lectures at Trinity College, Cambridge. *"Anna Karenina" and Other Essays* published by Chatto and Windus.

1969   *English Literature in Our Time and the University,* The Clark Lectures, and *Lectures in America,* with Q. D. Leavis, published by Chatto and Windus. F. R. and Q. D. Leavis give lectures in Italy. F. R. Leavis is visiting professor at the University of Wales and the University of Bristol.

1970 *Dickens the Novelist,* with Q. D. Leavis, published by Chatto and Windus. F. R. Leavis publishes articles in Ian Robinson's *The Human World* (1970–1974). Receives honorary degree from University of Aberdeen.

1972 *Nor Shall My Sword: Discourses on Pluralism, Compassion, and Social Hope* published by Chatto and Windus.

1973 Receives honorary degrees from Queen's University, Belfast and the University of Delhi.

1974 *Letters in Criticism,* edited by John Tasker, published by Chatto and Windus.

1975 *The Living Principle: "English" as a Discipline of Thought* published by Chatto and Windus.

1976 *Thought, Words, and Creativity: Art and Thought in Lawrence* published by Chatto and Windus.

1977 December, named a Companion of Honor.

1978 April 14, dies.

1981 March 17, Q. D. Leavis dies.

1982 *The Critic As Anti-Philosopher: Essays and Papers,* edited by G. S. Singh, published by Chatto and Windus.

1986 *Valuation in Criticism and Other Essays,* edited by G. S. Singh, published by Cambridge University Press.

1992 *More Letters in Criticism* by F. R. and Q. D. Leavis, edited by M. B. Kinch, published from Bradford on Avon.

1995 Ian MacKillop's *F. R. Leavis: A Life in Criticism* published by Chatto and Windus.

Chapter One

Life

Frank Raymond Leavis, arguably the greatest English literary critic of the twentieth century, was born at 64 Mill Road, Cambridge, England on July 14, 1895 to Harry and Kate Sarah Moore Leavis. Leavis believed that on his father's side his family was related to the family of duc de Lévis, Huguenots who fled France for England following the revocation of the Edict of Nantes and the St. Bartholomew's Day Massacre of 1572. The nineteenth-century Leavis family lived in the villages of Elm and Denver near Wisbech, 40 miles north of Cambridge on the Cambridgeshire/Norfolk border.[1]

Leavis's paternal grandfather Elihu, a piano-tuner, had three children: Frederick, Alice, and Harry. In 1881 the family (Elihu was widowed early) was living in the New Town area of Cambridge near Mill Road. Leavis's father served an apprenticeship as a shopkeeper in Cambridge and then moved to Broadwood's in London to learn the piano trade. In 1890 he returned to Cambridge and established a shop in Mill Road. He moved the business to premises on Regent Street opposite Downing College in 1901. He had married Kate Sarah Moore, who was nine years his senior. Originally from Bury St. Edmunds in Suffolk, she was a neighbor in the New Town area. Leavis described his father as "a Victorian radical. There was a fierce, Protestant conscience there, but it was divorced from any religious outlet"(qtd. in MacKillop, 29). According to biographer Ian MacKillop, Leavis's mother was easily hurt by her husband's scorn for religion (MacKillop, 29). Perhaps this parental conflict is the origin of Leavis's own theological skepticism yet deep valuation of a religious sense of life. The Leavises had three children: Ruth was two years older and Ralph Moore 18 months younger than Frank. Ralph, who like his brother served in the Friends' Ambulance Unit in World War I, inherited the family piano business.

Leavis began school at Eden Street Infants' School. In March 1903, a few months before his eighth birthday, he entered Paradise Street Higher Grade School, which he attended until April 1910. In 1907, the family moved to a house designed by Harry Leavis at 6 Chesterton Hall Crescent.[2] At least between October 1907 and May 1908, Leavis produced for his family the *Home Made Magazine,* which contained detailed nature descriptions. At school he gained distinctions in English and Religious Knowledge and was awarded "Mr Starr's Prize for English" at the City Guildhall on February 24, 1910 (MacKillop, 31).[3]

Harry Leavis was an energetic man, Liberal and republican in politics and rationalist in religion. He helped to establish the New Chesterton Institute, which ran societies such as a drama group for which he acted in *Pickwick Papers.* Family readings of Dickens were held each week. The family took a lively interest in gardening and local and natural history. In her candid and moving memoir "6, Chesterton Hall Crescent, and the early years," Leavis's niece, Mary Pitter, describes her uncle Frank as a rooted man who loved Cambridge and the natural world:

> He taught me my first lesson in appreciating beauty of form. I had spent my pocket money on a packet of nasturtium seeds which depicted both double and single flowers on the front. He pointed to the double flowers and remarked, "A beautiful natural form spoiled," and I saw at once what he meant. There was hardly a visit when he did not extend and educate my first steps in discernment and appreciation. The lessons learnt were given and received in a completely natural way, because this was all part of how he lived and what he believed.[4]

In the autumn of 1910, Leavis moved from Paradise Street to the Cambridge and County School. In the school debating society he argued against compulsory military training. Also, he won the school essay prize for "Little-Boy-Man," an essay about a butterfly collector.[5] It was at about this time that he began to read poetry seriously. Leavis, or his father, subscribed to the *English Review,* in which Leavis first encountered the stories of D. H. Lawrence. In July 1911 he won a scholarship to the Perse Grammar School, which he attended until the summer of 1914. During Leavis's time there, the headmaster was W. H. D. Rouse, general editor of the Loeb Classical Library. Rouse was famous for teaching classical languages by the Direct Method. Leavis recalled how, when he was late for school because of a flat bicycle tire, he had to describe in Greek how to mend a puncture. Drama also flourished at the school, and Leavis acted the title role in a scene from *Macbeth,* as well as the Gypsy Man in a dramatization of *The Wraggle-Taggle Gypsies.* He was an excellent student, especially in English, French, German, Greek, History, and Latin. As well, he played rugby for the school and was a fine swimmer and cross-country runner. However, he refused to join the Officer's Training Corps or the Boy Scouts.

In December 1913, Leavis took the scholarship examination at Emmanuel College in the University of Cambridge and won a £60 scholarship to read for the History Tripos. He began his university studies two months after war was declared and took his first examinations in June 1915. Military conscription was on the horizon. Leavis decided to withdraw from the university and, in the autumn of 1915, began training as a hospital orderly at a Quaker center in York. In a 1977 letter he told Michael Tanner:

> I couldn't be a pacifist (that word came in then); I knew that the Germans mustn't be allowed to win. . . . I joined the Friends Ambulance Unit. Stinking blankets and lice, and always a job to do that was too much for me. But after the Bloody Somme there could be no question for *anyone* who knew what modern war was like of joining the army.
>
> I didn't want to come home, and couldn't communicate with my father—whom I loved. (MacKillop, 39)

In York Leavis bought a copy of the World's Classics edition of John Milton's poems—the only book he carried in his pocket continuously between 1915 and 1919. He trained and served as a mess orderly, nursing orderly, and guard before beginning service abroad.

Leavis left York on June 25, 1916 and on July 8 sailed for France. On his 21st birthday he joined an ambulance train at Boulogne. The Battle of the Somme had been in progress for two weeks. From August 16 he spent 21 months working on Ambulance Train Number 5. Its purpose was to bring the wounded from casualty clearing stations to hospitals or hospital ships. The work involved nursing, cooking, and cleaning. AT5 (as it was known) was made up of assorted carriages with no connecting corridor. MacKillop quotes a letter of Leavis's in which he recalls that, "I used to carry cocoa [in buckets] along the roofs of French trains to men who would have died without it. The trains had overhead wires, and it was very easy to get your head caught" (MacKillop, 42). During Leavis's first six weeks, AT5 made 30 trips between Étaples and Calais, on one occasion loading 700 wounded aboard between 10 P.M. and 3 A.M. Medical personnel were also contaminated by poison gas breathed in from the combatants' uniforms. When the armistice occurred Leavis was in Paris, where the train was being repaired following a collision. Earlier it had been bombed. During Leavis's time aboard, it had traveled behind the lines all over Belgium and northern France carrying the wounded away from such battles as Ypres and Passchendaele.

Leavis returned home with a stammer, insomnia, and his digestion ruined. He was probably suffering from what is now known as post-traumatic stress disorder. During the 1920s he tried to overcome insomnia by running at night along the Ely Road. He taught himself Italian and learned passages of Dante, Paul Valéry, and Percy Bysshe Shelley's *Adonais* in attempts to take his mind off his memories of the war (MacKillop and Storer, 119). He admired the war poetry of Isaac Rosenberg, in particular the poem "Dead Man's Dump." In a 1964 letter to George A. Panichas, Leavis recalled:

> I see the faces of those boys who were with me at school as if it were last week and hear their voices. They began to appear in the "Roll of Honour" within a few months: Festubert, Loos, and then the Somme, where they were reaped in swathes. They were shot down over Ypres, and, having survived from the days of Kitchener's first army to the "victorious" battles of 1918, died of wounds—and of sickness after the Armistice. (qtd. in MacKillop, 46)

Fifty years later the war remained painfully and unforgettably vivid in Leavis's imagination. In a late lecture, "Wordsworth: The Creative Conditions," delivered at Bristol University in 1970, which he called "the best thing I've done" (MacKillop, 19), Leavis speaks of William Wordsworth's experience of the French Revolution in a way that could equally describe his own experience of World War I, if we read "World War I" for "Revolution":

> Earnest, responsible, and loyal by nature, he identified himself with the Revolution, and the Revolution developed in the way it did. He witnessed, close at hand, hopes frustrated, suffering entailed upon the innocent and helpless, and diverse kinds of human deterioration, he being very young. His own innocent assumptions and his exalted faith were brutally questioned by actualities; the Revolution, in the accepted phrase, devoured its children. . . .[6]

Although, like Wordsworth, Leavis "eludes" what he calls "the close confident knowledge aspired to by the modern biographer," as Wordsworth suffered from the French Revolution, so Leavis suffered from World War I:

> he suffered a moral and emotional crisis; the haunting question was, how could he reconcile himself to life? When we find him again, living in the country, he has—tacitly, at least—come to one decision: he has re-

nounced the centres and activities of political man and "the storm / of sorrow barricadoed evermore / within the walls of cities." And drawing on memories and habits of childhood and boyhood, he is bent on identifying the desired emotional-moral balance ("equipoise," the Wanderer calls it) with a devotion to "Nature"—. ("Wordsworth," 37)

For Leavis we might substitute "English" and "life" for "Nature," but it is clear that the effect of World War I was more profound upon him than the effect of the French Revolution upon Wordsworth. In both cases, Leavis's words ring with a painful truth: "But the trauma is there . . . 'the painful pressure,' the compulsion to 'feed on disquiet' is there" ("Wordsworth," 37).

Leavis was demobilized on January 2, 1918. He returned to Cambridge to complete part one of the History Tripos. He had only five months to prepare for his examinations. During the summer of 1919 he decided to switch from History to the new English Tripos. He was motivated to do so by his love of poetry, in particular T. S. Eliot's "The Love Song of J. Alfred Prufrock" and "Portrait of a Lady." For Leavis, Eliot represented modern poetry that had broken free of the escapist poetry of the Victorians, Edwardians, and Georgians. Leavis became interested in J. Middleton Murry's literary criticism in the *Athenaeum* and soon afterward in T. S. Eliot's *The Sacred Wood* (1920). In October 1919, he registered to study "English Literature: Modern and Medieval" as part one of the English Tripos. Two part ones (in Leavis's case, in History and English) could be taken to complete an honors degree.

When Leavis registered there was still no English Department or faculty in Cambridge University. Tutorial supervision and lectures were provided within colleges by Directors of Studies. Sir Arthur Quiller-Couch ("Q" was his pen name), appointed King Edward VII Professor of English Literature in 1912, gave university lectures on literature from the Renaissance period on. He was to become Leavis's Ph.D. supervisor. H. Munro Chadwick lectured on Anglo-Saxon and G. G. Coulton on medieval literature for the university. It was possible to attend lectures given at colleges other than one's own. The lecturers Leavis found most interesting during his years of undergraduate and graduate study were Mansfield Forbes and I. A. Richards. Their close reading or "practical criticism" helped Leavis to base his own criticism in careful reading and first-hand judgments of individual works of literature. There were also special series of lectures, such as Trinity College's Clark Lectures in which J. Middleton Murry lectured on John Keats and William Shakespeare (1925), T. S. Eliot on the Metaphysical Poets (1926), and E. M. Forster on aspects of the novel (1927). Leavis experienced fully the original "Cambridge English," devised by Quiller-Couch, Chadwick, and Forbes, with which his own name was to become closely associated.

Between October 1919 and May 1921 Leavis had to prepare for six examinations: English Literature, Life and Thought (1350–1603); History of English Literature (1603–); Shakespeare, including passages (some unattributed) for comment, and questions on language, meter, literary history, and criticism; Special Period of Literature (1789–1870); Special Subject: Tragedy, and History of Literary Criticism.[7] Commenting on these papers, Ian MacKillop remarks that, "Cambridge English became a home for close reading, but from the beginning, even in the typographical look of the papers, its examinations urged an intimate connection with analysis and history" (MacKillop, 59). At the end of May 1921, Leavis had to write these six examinations in a week. He would later call such examination performance "stand-and-deliver against the clock."[8] On May 13 Leavis's father was fatally injured in a motorcycle accident. Leavis visited his father daily, later telling D. W. Harding that "he drew on his wartime experience . . . of giving what care and attention was still possible for badly wounded men for whom no further medical treatment was useful or available" (MacKillop, 69). On May 20 Harry Leavis slipped into a coma. He died on May 22, the day of Leavis's first examination. His funeral was held on the day his son wrote the examination on tragedy. Leavis's first class in the English Tripos was announced on June 21.

On the recommendation of Sir Arthur Quiller-Couch and Mansfield D. Forbes, Leavis was awarded an Emmanuel Research Studentship, valued at £150, to undertake graduate work toward a Ph.D. Quiller-Couch was happy to supervise his thesis and sympathetically impressed by the courage Leavis had shown through his recent ordeals. In his letter of reference Quiller-Couch wrote:

> I hadn't the faintest compunction in signing him up for a First—even apart from the pluck of the whole performance, which was astonishing. (I lost my father in my last year at Oxford, and know what it means.) I suppose Leavis was too shy to worry me personally for advice: and you know that under pretty constant bombardment by those who are not shy I haven't the time to look up those who are. But I should be happy to make amends if given the chance of supervising his work for a research degree. He has suggested a very good subject, and I know enough of him to be pretty sure he would make a good fist of it. (MacKillop, 70)

Leavis wrote to thank Forbes for his support when he received the award.

For the Ph.D. a long dissertation had to be submitted within three years of registration. Leavis's title was "The Relationship of Journalism to Literature: Studied in the Rise and Earlier Development of the Press in England." Never published, the thesis can be read in the Cambridge University Library. In a note attached to it, Leavis advises the eager researcher against making a copy of the thesis since it was written before the English scholarly industry had begun. Quiller-Couch was interested in journalism (his King Edward VII Professorship was funded by Fleet Street) and had been a serious journalist himself. The bulk of Leavis's thesis concentrated on eighteenth-century literature. Quiller-Couch told I. A. Richards that "[n]o small part" of his work of supervision "was steering him [Leavis] clear of nervous breakdown. . . . I was extremely anxious about him, to the last moment" (qtd. in MacKillop, 71). Leavis surveyed journalism from the Elizabethan period to the middle of the eighteenth century. The thesis, externally examined by George Saintsbury, was approved on November 18, 1924, and his degree conferred the following week.

During his doctoral work, Leavis had continued to attend undergraduate lectures, in particular I. A. Richards's series, "Practical Criticism," at which Mansfield Forbes was frequently present. Both lecturers encouraged students to develop their own judgments of short poems. Besides the importance of first-hand response and judgment ("a judgement is personal or it is nothing,"[9] Leavis would later say), Leavis was interested in Forbes's idea of "complexity"—of different strains of style, poetic convention, or tradition being blended or juxtaposed within an individual poem. Though seeking individual expression, a poet would reveal his influences and origins. Often, of course, such derivations would not be transcended. The critic's task was to identify originality and derivativeness, to discriminate between falseness and sentimentality and authenticity and sincerity. Forbes and Richards both stressed the importance of "reading out" poetry, an aural as well as a written art. They experimented in reading out the same poem to their lecture audience but in each other's absence so as not to be influenced by each other's reading. Rhythm, tone, and inflection were as important in poetry as word choice and image. Despite the influence of Imagism, poetry was not, like painting, a primarily visual art.

In 1925, Leavis joined Stanley Bennett, his colleague and friend at Emmanuel, as a college lecturer and freelance supervisor. He gave a

course of lectures on "Literature and Society from the Restoration to the
Death of Johnson." Also, he was hired by Hilda Murray, Director of
Studies in Languages at Girton College, to supervise English students
there. She was a daughter of Sir James Murray, editor of the *Oxford English
Dictionary,* and to Leavis she was "daughter of the *Dictionary*"
(MacKillop, 93–94). Through his supervisory work at Girton, Leavis
was to meet his future wife, Queenie Dorothy Roth, eldest daughter of a
North London Orthodox Jewish family, who came up to Cambridge in
October 1925 at the age of 18.

In his second year as a college lecturer, Leavis added a course on "Modern Poetry" to his series of lectures on literature of the eighteenth century.
During the summer of 1926, he tried to obtain a copy, through a Cambridge bookseller, of James Joyce's *Ulysses* for use in a course he was considering. The novel had been banned since its publication in 1922. Leavis
only wished to order a copy for himself, but the bookseller inquired about
obtaining an additional copy for students' library use. In the event, the
Director of Public Prosecutions wrote to the vice-chancellor of the university, who interviewed Dr. Leavis. Leavis admitted to referring to *Ulysses* in
a lecture but said that he had no intention of requiring students to buy the
book. The event became a minor cause célèbre in Cambridge, the university newspaper referring to a "Leavis Prize for Pornography."

At this time (October 1926) when the university was divided into
faculties, an English faculty was established. In January 1927, Leavis
was offered a probationary faculty lectureship for two years. It was not a
tenurable position. During the academic year 1927–1928 he gave lectures on "Twentieth-Century Poetry" and "Critics and Critical Problems." The following year, he added a course on "Prose, with Passages
for Criticism." In spring 1928, Leavis was disappointed not to be offered
one of three new faculty lectureships, especially since two colleagues,
who had graduated more recently than he, were offered lectureships.

In autumn 1927 Leavis met Queenie Dorothy Roth. She was almost
21 and he was 32. She may have helped him to begin to write again (he
had not written much since completing his doctoral dissertation three
years earlier). However, writing in the *Cambridge Review* in criticism of
King's College Fellow and English Faculty member F. L. Lucas's attitude toward T. S. Eliot led to Leavis's unpopularity with the Cambridge
English establishment. Lucas was part of the Bloomsbury group that
included J. M. Keynes, Lytton Strachey, and Virginia Woolf. Leavis
argued in his "T. S. Eliot: A Reply to the Condescending" that Lucas was
insufficiently serious about literature. Q. D. Roth was in her final year of

undergraduate study when she and Leavis met. In spring 1928, she received a starred first class degree. As Leavis had earlier, she went on to doctoral study. Supervised by I. A. Richards and Mansfield Forbes, her thesis was published as *Fiction and the Reading Public* (1932). In some respects, it followed Leavis's own doctoral work in literary anthropology or sociology but provided a fuller investigation of the modern period. Leavis and Queenie Roth became engaged in February 1929. Her parents were so shocked by her decision to marry out of the Jewish faith that they broke off relations with their daughter. Fortunately for the couple, who married on September 16 in the Cambridge Registry Office, Leavis's probationary contract was given a two-year extension until October 1931.

The Leavises spent their honeymoon cycling and walking in Norfolk. In her "Memoir" published in G. S. Singh's *F. R. Leavis: A Literary Biography,* Q. D. Leavis describes briefly a never repeated experience of sailing with Leavis on the Norfolk Broads, "The Norfolk Broads. Our honeymoon. Never again" (Singh, 20). Returning from their honeymoon, the couple settled in a small house on Leys Road, which Leavis had bought for £1,000. They referred to their home as "The Criticastery." There they held regular Friday teas attended by such students and colleagues as Ronald Bottrall, Gordon Fraser, Denys Harding, L. C. Knights, Ian Parsons, Denys Thompson, and Ludwig Wittgenstein. Toward the end of 1929, Leavis's mother died.

Following his marriage Leavis completed his essay "English Poetry and the Modern World: A Study of the Current Situation," which was to become the first chapter of *New Bearings in English Poetry.* It appeared in the French journal *Cahiers du Sud* in October 1930. Also in 1930, a student of Leavis's at St. John's College, Gordon Fraser, established the Minority Press that published several of Leavis's early writings. As Fraser remarked, "At the age of nineteen I was Leavis's student and his publisher: a friendship that was to last fifty years" (MacKillop, 113). Both *Mass Civilisation and Minority Culture* and *D. H. Lawrence* appeared from the Minority Press that year, the year of Lawrence's death. With Leavis's assistance, Minority Press published Ronald Bottrall's first volume, *The Loosening and Other Poems* (1931). In January 1931 Leavis learned that his probationary lectureship would not be renewed. In the middle of the same month, his enthusiastic review of William Empson's *Seven Types of Ambiguity* (1930) appeared in the *Cambridge Review.* Empson had been expelled from Cambridge in 1929 when contraceptives were found in his room.

In March the Leavises returned to the Leavis family home at 6 Chesterton Hall Crescent. In the autumn of 1931, without a lectureship, Leavis told Ronald Bottrall, "I'm faced with a void" (MacKillop, 127). He was not invited to be an examiner for the English Tripos, and he even lost his teaching at Emmanuel and St. John's following a quarrel with Stanley Bennett.

Q. D. Leavis completed her doctoral thesis, "Fiction and the Reading Public: a Study in Social Anthropology"; her oral defense took place on November 8, 1931. Her external examiner was E. M. Forster. Despite the reservations of her supervisor, I. A. Richards, the thesis was quickly accepted for publication by Chatto and Windus. Ian Parsons at Chatto and Windus became the Leavises' principal publisher for the next 50 years. Q. D. Leavis received a research scholarship worth £150 for further study following her Ph.D. At the beginning of 1932 Leavis was able to offer a lecture series as a freelance. This lecture series, "Tradition and Development in English Poetry (with texts)," became the basis of *Revaluation* (1936). *New Bearings in English Poetry* and *Fiction and the Reading Public* were published by Chatto and Windus in February and April respectively.

Later in 1931 plans for *Scrutiny: A Quarterly Review* were made in discussions at Chesterton Hall Crescent. *Scrutiny* grew out of meetings of young researchers in English who were interested, like the Leavises, in the relation between a vital literature and society. The group included L. C. Knights (whose *Drama and Society in the Age of Jonson* appeared in 1937); Eric McCormick, a New Zealander working on his country's literature; Dutch Sri Lankan, E. F. C. Ludowyk; Iqbal Singh; Donald Culver; and Carlos Peacock. McCormick and Singh wished to start a D. H. Lawrence–inspired journal called *The Phoenix*. Leavis, however, wanted something of wider scope. Culver suggested considering the American journal *Symposium* as a model. On May 15, 1932, the first issue of *Scrutiny* appeared under the editorship of Knights and Culver. Leavis supplied advice, and financial backing from the sale of his Leys Road house. A model for *Scrutiny* was provided by the *Calendar of Modern Letters,* which ran from March 1925 to July 1927. Its fearlessness and high standards impressed Leavis, who chose and introduced a selection from it called *Towards Standards of Criticism,* published by Wishart and Company in 1933. The first print run of *Scrutiny* was 500 copies. It sold at 10 shillings for four issues. Eventually the print run rose as high as 1,400. During 1933 Leavis paid as much as £200 from his own pocket toward *Scrutiny's* establishment. Unlike the *Calendar of Modern Letters,* which paid its contributors and collapsed after two and a half years, *Scrutiny*'s contributors were unpaid, surely the reason, together with the Leavises' dedication, that the journal survived for 21 years. Leavis became an editor with the third number in November 1932. Also, *How to Teach Reading: A Primer for Ezra Pound* was published by the Minority Press in 1932.

In 1933 Leavis published *For Continuity,* a selection of his *Scrutiny* articles together with *Mass Civilisation and Minority Culture* and *D. H. Lawrence,* from the Minority Press. Also, with Denys Thompson he produced what he called an "opuscule," strongly indebted to *Fiction and the Reading Public,* called *Culture and Environment: The Training of Critical Awareness.* It was published by Chatto and Windus for use in schools. Denys Thompson had become a master at Gresham's School. He later founded the *Use of English* journal. Leavis's influence reached the schools through activities and connections of this kind. Chatto and Windus published a selection of essays from *Scrutiny* called *Determinations* in 1934.

The Leavises' first son, Ralph, was born in January 1934. Early in life he suffered from celiac disease and had to spend some time in a London hospital. Following the end of his probationary lectureship in October 1931 and loss of supervisory work at Emmanuel and St. John's, Leavis found supervisory work at Downing College through his friend William Cuttle, who he had met at Emmanuel and who had become a fellow in Classics at Downing. Leavis was appointed a supervisor in June 1931 and Director of Studies in English in December at the meager stipend of five guineas a term. This was the beginning of an association that was to last for 33 years. Though Leavis was not offered a university lectureship on the deaths of Aubrey Attwater in 1935 and Mansfield Forbes in January 1936, he was appointed to a college lectureship at Downing worth £125 per annum in March 1936. Through the support of Sir Arthur Quiller-Couch, Leavis was finally appointed to a part-time three year probationary university lectureship in October 1936 (MacKillop, 159). What Leavis called his "Six Years War" with the university's English Faculty had ended, at least for the time being.

At Christmas, Downing College withdrew Leavis's lectureship and elected him to a college fellowship instead. His salary was increased to £200 per annum. Leavis attracted excellent students to the college who did well in the Tripos examinations. In 1934, Cuttle and Leavis founded the college's Doughty Society "to encourage the study of literature in all its branches, classical and modern" (MacKillop, 163). Successful students who contributed to *Scrutiny* and in some cases assisted Leavis at Downing included: Marius Bewley, R. G. Cox, D. J. Enright, Boris Ford, Wilfred Mellers, and Geoffrey Walton. Leavis dedicated his second book on English poetry, *Revaluation: Tradition and Development in English Poetry*, published by Chatto and Windus in 1936, to Downing College. In *Revaluation*, based upon lecture series he had given, Leavis was, as MacKillop puts it, "turning to the historic stream of English poetry, using the lectures to establish new bearings in older English poetry" (MacKillop, 170).

Through this period, Leavis had been working intermittently on a book tentatively titled "Authority and Method," later "Judgement and Analysis." Though it was never completed, material from this work, often used in Leavis's lectures, appeared in *Scrutiny* and finally in *The Living Principle* (1975). Through the early 1930s, Leavis's sympathy moved increasingly from T. S. Eliot to D. H. Lawrence, while his March 1935 *Scrutiny* review of I. A. Richards's *Coleridge on Imagination* revealed the degree of Leavis's separation from his early mentor. Titled "Dr. Richards, Bentham, and Coleridge," the review criticized the "scientistic" way in which Richards had attempted to assimilate Samuel Taylor Coleridge to Jeremy Bentham. Leavis would later (1950) introduce an edition of John Stuart Mill's writings on Bentham and Coleridge for Chatto and Windus. Separation from Richards meant separation from Richards's protegé William Empson, whose poems in *Cambridge Poetry 1929* and *Seven Types of Ambiguity* Leavis had admired.

In June 1937, Leavis spoke on Isaac Rosenberg's poetry at the Whitechapel Gallery in east London on the opening of an exhibition of Rosenberg's paintings and drawings. Rosenberg's *Collected Works*, edited by Denys Harding and Gordon Bottomley, had appeared earlier in the month. Leavis reviewed Rosenberg's *Collected Works* in *Scrutiny* in September.

The Leavises' daughter, Kate Laura, was born in September 1939. Her brother Ralph was becoming a musical prodigy. He completed a piano concerto at the age of ten. Though World War II was never mentioned in *Scrutiny* (Robinson 1992, 12), with contributors on war service the 1940s was a difficult time for *Scrutiny* and for the Leavises. Q. D. Leavis's mother and sister were killed in the blitz in December 1940, just when there was a possibility of family reconciliation. Her father, Morris Roth, survived and came to know his grandchildren. A second son, Lawrence Robin, was born in December 1944. In 1946 Q. D. Leavis was diagnosed as suffering from breast cancer. During treatment,

she received radiation burns. The same year, Ralph was sent to Darting-
ton Hall school in Devon to study music. Leavis's lectureship (for "part
work") was extended in 1939. He was finally offered a full-time university lectureship in 1947, 20 years after his initial probationary appointment.

A series on education begun in *Scrutiny* in September 1940 with
"Education and the University: A Sketch for an 'English School' " and
followed by "Education and the University: Criticism and Comment,"
"Education and the University: (3) Literary Studies," and "Considera-
tions at a Critical Time" emerged, in revised form, as *Education & The
University: A Sketch for an "English School"* from Chatto and Windus in
1943. Leavis added "T. S. Eliot's Later Poetry"; an essay on "The Dry
Salvages," which he had recently reviewed; *How to Teach Reading;* and
Mass Civilisation and Minority Culture as appendices. Dedicated to
William Cuttle, the book contained the epigraph, "Collaboration, a
matter of differences as well as agreements. . . ." Basing his proposals on
his own work at Downing, Leavis was also preparing for educational
opportunities that the postwar world might bring. He believed from
first to last that the "English School" should be a liaison center within
the university; its members should support and be the nucleus of a creative minority that should provide the best consciousness of the age and
fight to keep alive a culture and its values.

Leavis's interest in fiction and prose increased in this period as he
moved toward the publication of *The Great Tradition: George Eliot, Henry
James, and Joseph Conrad* (1948), which he thought of as "New Bearings
in English Fiction" (MacKillop, 252), and *John Stuart Mill on Bentham
and Coleridge* (1950). In 1947 he began a series in *Scrutiny,* The Novel as
Dramatic Poem, with a piece on *Hard Times* that was reprinted at the
end of *The Great Tradition.* A link between his educational and literary
interests is provided by an essay, written in 1946 but not published in
Scrutiny until 1949, titled "Mill, Beatrice Webb, and the 'English
School,' " which became the introduction to *John Stuart Mill on Bentham
and Coleridge.* Beatrice Webb in *My Apprenticeship* (1926) indicated how
she had come to understand human society through the help of Herbert
Spencer and the great novelists.

After the death, in 1944, of Sir Arthur Quiller-Couch, Basil Willey
was appointed to the King Edward VII Chair of English Literature in
1946. It was a position that Leavis would have filled with distinction. In
this period, Leavis was exploring the nature of tragedy in his teaching
and in an essay he published in 1944 called "Tragedy and the 'Medium.' "

In 1949, Harold Mason, an Oxford classicist and contributor to *Scrutiny*, became additional Director of English Studies at Downing College, where Leavis's work had been particularly heavy since the end of World War II. Mason was at Downing from 1949 until 1955. The Leavis family moved from Chesterton Hall Crescent to Newton Road in 1951.

Leavis's next book was *The Common Pursuit*, published by Chatto and Windus in 1952. It contained 24 essays, mostly from *Scrutiny* but also from *Kenyon Review* and *Sewanee Review*. The essays ranged in subject from Eliot and Lawrence to Jonathan Swift, Alexander Pope and Samuel Johnson, John Bunyan, Shakespeare, "Literature and Society," and "Sociology and Literature." The title, taken from Eliot's "The Function of Criticism," indicates Leavis's lifelong endeavor, "the common pursuit of true judgement." But the opening purpose of the book was to deal with Eliot's British Academy retraction of his earlier criticisms of Milton. Leavis originally thought of calling the book *Mr. Eliot and Milton and Other Essays* (MacKillop, 265).

Scrutiny came to an end in 1953. Earlier, in 1950, Leavis had had a sharp correspondence with the editor of the *Times Literary Supplement*, Alan Pryce-Jones, over the issue of failing to notice *Scrutiny* in a review of contemporary literary journals. Sustaining *Scrutiny*, without institutional support, was financially and emotionally draining for the Leavises, who had worked tirelessly for it for 21 years. One of the last straws may have been the prospect that contributors would divide their efforts between *Scrutiny* and Boris Ford's soon-to-be-launched *Pelican Guide to English Literature*. Ten years later *Scrutiny* was reprinted by Cambridge University Press with a Retrospect by Leavis.

D. H. Lawrence: Novelist was published by Chatto and Windus in 1955. It incorporated several of Leavis's recent inquiries into the novel as dramatic poem. Studies of *St. Mawr, The Rainbow,* and *Women in Love* had appeared in this series in *Scrutiny*. In a letter to his publisher, Ian Parsons, Leavis spoke of his work as a mediator in the age of Eliot and Lawrence, the greatest poet and novelist of the period (MacKillop, 286). Leavis's view of Lawrence's novels had changed considerably in the 25 years since his Minority Press pamphlet of 1930. There he had praised *Lady Chatterley's Lover,* which he now had little time for, and written of the difficulty of *The Rainbow* and *Women in Love*. Studies of these novels, which Leavis now saw as the center of Lawrence's achievement, formed the core of *D. H. Lawrence: Novelist*. Lawrence, for Leavis, represented the culmination of "the great tradition" delineated in his earlier book.

About 1958, a bitter breach occurred between Ralph Leavis, who had taken a first class at Oxford, and his mother. Though Leavis continued to visit his son in Oxford whenever possible, relations between mother and son ceased. During 1957, Q. D. Leavis had been seriously ill as a consequence of her earlier cancer treatment. The same year, a former student, Morris Shapira, who had been supervising at Downing since 1954, became Leavis's assistant at Downing. In 1958, Kate Leavis followed her brother Ralph to Oxford. In the early 1960s, the Leavises' son Robin won an Exhibition (scholarship) to Clare College, Cambridge. Leavis was appointed University Reader in English in May 1959. At about this time he was considering a possible book on "The Critical Function" that would incorporate essays previously published in *Scrutiny* on Johnson, Coleridge, and Matthew Arnold as critics but would also include chapters on Eliot and Lawrence.

The decade of the 1960s was difficult for Leavis. In the early 1960s he refused to join what he called the "orthodoxy of enlightenment" in defense of Lawrence's *Lady Chatterley's Lover,* for the publication of which Penguin Books was tried for obscenity. Downing College commissioned a painting of Leavis by Peter Greenham (which now graces the cover of MacKillop's biography) to honor him on the occasion of his retirement, which was due to take place in September 1962. However, several problems occurred in the period surrounding his retirement. Leavis the controversialist emerged most completely in his February 1962 Richmond Lecture "Two Cultures? The Significance of C. P. Snow," a devastating response to Snow's Rede Lecture, "The Two Cultures and the Scientific Revolution" (1959). Leavis's lecture was published in *The Spectator* and later as a book by Chatto and Windus. In the lecture, Leavis attacked Snow's advocacy of what Leavis would thereafter refer to as our "technologico-Benthamite" age. In July 1964 he resigned his honorary fellowship at Downing because of the college's appointment of Brian Vickers as a fellow in English, its failure to renew the Directorship of English Studies of his assistant Morris Shapira beyond 1965, and its failure to consult Leavis in either case. In March 1966, he broke with a group of former students and colleagues (in particular John Newton, Ralph and Jean Gooder, and Morris Shapira), who had established an F. R. Leavis Lectureship Trust, over misunderstandings surrounding the appointment of Harold Mason to the lectureship.[10]

All ties with Cambridge University were severed by October 1966, so that when he was invited in 1967 by Trinity College to give the Clark

Lectures, he was returning to the University as the outsider he, in many ways, had always been. There is a story from the early 1960s, when Leavis was at the height of his popularity as a literary critic, that a group of Oxford University students wrote to him about the possibility of their transferring to Cambridge since English at Oxford was so dull. Leavis wondered how he could help them get into Cambridge since he was unable to get into Cambridge himself (MacKillop and Storer, 269). In March 1964 Leavis had delivered the Chichele Lecture at All Souls College, Oxford on Charles Dickens's *Little Dorrit,* one of his finest studies of the novel as dramatic poem, that would appear in *Dickens the Novelist* (1970). When he was nominated for the Chair of Poetry at Oxford in January 1961, the slogan "Leavis for Professor of Poetry" appeared on Oxford walls.

The Leavises moved from Newton Road to a smaller house in Bulstrode Gardens after Christmas 1962. Leavis's retirement from Cambridge University and separation from Downing College provided increased opportunities for the Leavises to travel. In autumn 1965 they gave lectures and seminars in Finland at the invitation of the British Council. The following October they visited Cornell and Harvard universities, where Leavis gave lectures on Eliot and Yeats, as well as a follow-up to his Richmond Lecture called "Luddites? *or* There is Only One Culture," while Q. D. Leavis lectured on *Wuthering Heights.* These lectures were published as *Lectures in America* by Chatto and Windus in 1969. The same year Chatto and Windus published Leavis's Clark Lectures (1967) as *English Literature in Our Time and the University.* They were dedicated "To the Memory of H. Munro Chadwick & Mansfield D. Forbes to whom the world owes more than it knows." These two men were, in Leavis's judgment, the true founders of Cambridge English. Leavis had dedicated an earlier volume of his essays, *"Anna Karenina" and Other Essays* (1967), also published by Chatto and Windus, "To The University of York," which had invited him to become a visiting professor in 1965. In 1969 the Leavises gave lectures in Italy arranged by G. S. Singh, professor of Italian at Queen's University, Belfast. Professor Singh and the Leavises' son Robin were to become the Leavises' literary executors. During this visit Leavis enjoyed meeting the Italian poet Eugenio Montale, whose poem *Xenia* Leavis had discussed in *The Listener* (December 16, 1971). Also, during 1969 and 1970 Leavis was visiting professor at the University of Wales and University of Bristol.

In October 1970, the centenary year of Dickens's death, the Leavises' *Dickens the Novelist* was published by Chatto and Windus. F. R. Leavis discussed *Dombey and Son, Hard Times,* and *Little Dorrit,* while Q. D. Leavis discussed *David Copperfield, Bleak House,* and *Great Expectations.* The book contained the following dedication:

> We dedicate this book to each other as proof, along with *Scrutiny* (of which for twenty-one years we sustained the main burden and the responsibility), of forty years and more of daily collaboration in living, university teaching, discussion of literature and the social and cultural context from which literature is born, and above all, devotion to the fostering of that true respect for creative writing, creative minds and, English literature being in question, the English tradition, without which literary criticism can have no validity and no life.

The novels studied were those the Leavises regarded as the best of Dickens's novels. Early in 1970, after the book had been sent to the publisher, Q. D. Leavis was seriously ill and spent six weeks in hospital.

During 1970 Leavis delivered the bicentenary lecture on Wordsworth at the University of Bristol, "Wordsworth: the Creative Conditions."[11] In 1972, he published with Chatto and Windus six of what he called his "field-performances" (MacKillop, 374) or works of "higher-pamphleteering" as *Nor Shall My Sword: Discourses on Pluralism, Compassion, and Social Hope.* These included "Two Cultures? The Significance of Lord Snow," the original Richmond Lecture of 1962, and "Luddites? *or* There is Only One Culture," which had been delivered at Harvard in 1966. The other four pieces, " 'English,' Unrest, and Continuity"; " 'Literarism' versus 'Scientism': The Misconception and the Menace"; "Pluralism, Compassion, and Social Hope"; and "Elites, Oligarchies, and an Educated Public," were delivered as lectures at the University of Wales, University of Bristol, and University of York; the last two appeared in a journal begun by Ian Robinson in 1970, called *The Human World* (1970–1974).

The Human World was a strong supporter, and publisher, of Leavis. In May 1971 it published a review article called "The Third Realm" that discussed "ten years' work by F. R. Leavis."[12] (The *third realm* was a term that Leavis had used in his Richmond Lecture to describe the place, neither wholly private nor wholly public, in which individual minds meet in "the collaborative-creative process" of literary criticism.[13]) Leavis is described as "the first critical mind of our age" ("Third Realm," 71), and his career is briefly reviewed. "Dr. Leavis's first reputation is still that of the revaluer of our literature for our age, the critic who more than any other has given a coherent picture of the great English authors and their

relative importance" ("Third Realm," 72). Leavis is seen in the Arnold
tradition as widening his literary criticism into a significant criticism of
life. In his work on literature as criticism of life, Leavis has become "a
very considerable philosopher of language" ("Third Realm," 74) whose
most important critical judgment was made in *D. H. Lawrence: Novelist*
(1955): "that our time, in literature, may fairly be called the age of
D. H. Lawrence and T. S. Eliot: the two, in creative preeminence, I
think . . . will be seen in retrospect to dominate the age together"
("Third Realm," 81). However, "Nobody has succeeded them. . . . The
present age of English literature is the age of Dr. Leavis. Who else
among our men of letters can show us where and what we are?" ("Third
Realm," 81),

> [Leavis] confers on us the power to see the truth, the truth in our world,
> of the writers he depends on. Eliot, writing of himself, defines Leavis's
> kind of greatness:
>> And what there is to conquer
>> By strength and submission, has already been discovered
>> Once or twice, or several times, by men one cannot hope
>> To emulate—but there is no competition—
>> There is only the fight to recover what has been lost
>> And found and lost again and again: and now, under conditions
>> That seem unpropitious.
>
> ("Third Realm," 85)

In 1974, Chatto and Windus published Leavis's *Letters in Criticism,*
edited by John Tasker, letters of Leavis's written and published between
1932 and 1973. Eighteen years later M. B. Kinch published *More Letters
in Criticism* by F. R. and Q. D. Leavis. *The Living Principle: "English" As a
Discipline of Thought* appeared from Chatto and Windus in 1975. It
opened with a section, "Thought, Language, and Objectivity," a consideration of literature as thought, followed by "Judgement and Analysis,"
material originally intended for "Authority and Method" that had been
used as lecture material as early as the 1930s and published in *Scrutiny* in
the late 1940s and early 1950s. The book concluded with a detailed
analysis (over 100 pages) of T. S. Eliot's *Four Quartets* in which Leavis
discussed what he perceived as Eliot's divided inner self and distrust of
creativity. It was a remarkable book published by a man in his 80th year
still intensely engaged in trying to get right what it meant to read literature seriously. But it was not his last. For Leavis, Eliot and Lawrence

were the twentieth century's major poet and major novelist; he wished to define as fully as he could what Lawrence offered us as "thought" in his creative writing. *Thought, Words, and Creativity: Art and Thought in Lawrence* appeared in 1976. Both books were published by Chatto and Windus, now Leavis's publisher for over forty years. These books introduce terms that Leavis had not used previously: *nisus*, meaning "will," and a German word, *ahnung*, that means "instinct." Also, in his discussions of language he drew upon three books that he had found particularly helpful: R. G. Collingwood's *The Idea of Nature;* Marjorie Grene's *The Knower and the Known*; and Michael Polanyi's *Knowing and Being.* As he explored the relations between language, criticism, and philosophy he returned to an interest in Wittgenstein, who he had first met in Cambridge in 1929. This led to a reminiscence, "Memories of Wittgenstein," edited and published by Ian Robinson in *The Human World* in 1973.

Leavis's 80th birthday was recognized in a radio program called "Leavis at Eighty: What Has His Influence Been?" (MacKillop, 403). Also, his birthday was recognized by a series of articles in *New Universities Quarterly.* Leavis responded to a piece in this series by Michael Tanner called "Literature and Philosophy" in an essay called "Mutually Necessary" about the need for both literary criticism *and* philosophy. This essay was reprinted in a posthumous volume that contained some of Leavis's later writings, *The Critic as Anti-Philosopher,* edited by G. S. Singh.

In the summer of 1977, Leavis, now 82, was ill. He suffered from occasional blackouts and was subject to confusion. He ate little but would take brandy; he said that he longed for oblivion. He cherished a photograph of his son Ralph. At the end of 1977, he was named a Companion of Honor, "for services to the study of English Literature" (MacKillop, 409). He died on Friday, April 14, 1978; his funeral was held at the Cambridge crematorium on Huntingdon Road. Q. D., Kate, and Robin Leavis were among those in attendance. Q. D. Leavis kept a death-bed photograph of her husband but burned the letters he had written to her. Almost three years after her husband, she died on March 17, 1981. As their mutual dedication to *Dickens the Novelist* indicated, their marriage had provided the fullest realization of the collaboration they had both sought. Q. D. Leavis saw her husband as he saw Hopkins, as "a man of high intelligence, fine human perception, irresistible charm and complete integrity" (see Singh, 223).

Chapter Two

New Bearings in English Criticism: 1924–1932

When F. R. Leavis's Clark Lectures (1967) were published by Chatto and Windus in 1969 as *English Literature in Our Time and the University*, the volume contained the dedication "To the Memory of H. Munro Chadwick & Mansfield D. Forbes to whom the world owes more than it knows." As much as T. S. Eliot or I. A. Richards, Chadwick and Forbes represented for Leavis twin inspirations for his own critical work. Chadwick stood for a sense of English literature and cultural history that involved a full understanding of the society from which culture and literature emerged. As Q. D. Leavis put it in her 1947 *Scrutiny* article, "Professor Chadwick and English Studies," "[h]e [Chadwick] showed how literary and linguistic studies could be made most profitable by successfully correlating them with their social background."[1] Forbes, on the other hand, inspired Leavis in the intelligent close reading of literary texts for which Leavis himself became famous. Together Chadwick and Forbes represented the best of the original Cambridge English in which Leavis grew up. With Quiller-Couch, Chadwick and Forbes were, in fact, the founders of Cambridge English during World War I. Theirs was the Cambridge English to which Leavis returned after the war to complete his undergraduate studies. His move from History to English in 1919 was the most important decision of his career.

It was for Quiller-Couch that Leavis wrote his doctoral thesis, between 1921 and 1924, on "The Relationship of Journalism to Literature: Studied in the Rise and Earlier Development of the Press in England." Both the Chadwick (the relation of literature to society) and the Forbes (the close reading of texts) elements, inextricably linked in this early phase of Leavis's criticism, are evident throughout his work.

Leavis's achievement in *New Bearings in English Poetry* (1932) and *Revaluation* (1936) is to have presented a major reorientation in the understanding of the history of English poetry. This could not have been accomplished without the attendant cultural investigation undertaken in such works as his doctoral thesis; *Mass Civilisation and Minority Cul-*

ture (1930), in which he appears to have been working alongside Q. D. Leavis as she prepared her doctoral thesis, *Fiction and the Reading Public* (1932); or *Culture and Environment* (1933), in which he and Denys Thompson drew upon Q. D. Leavis's work. Besides, the emergence of *Scrutiny,* in 1932, drew together the Leavises' cultural and critical interests. In an effort to show how the two elements identified with Chadwick and Forbes interact and support each other in Leavis's criticism, I will, in this chapter, attempt a careful reading of the four full-length works completed by Leavis between 1924 and 1932.

Returning from World War I, Leavis sought physical and spiritual health. He found spiritual health in the best examples of English literature. At the close of his Introduction to his Ph.D. thesis, Leavis presents a perception to which he adhered throughout his life as a critic: "A healthy literature must grow out of life as it is lived: it must embody the thoughts, the concerns, the spiritual forces that are moulding a community."[2] Careful analysis of quotation together with an understanding of the vital relation between "[a] healthy literature" and its social and cultural environment are immediately evident in the Introduction to Leavis's first sustained piece of critical writing.

In his opening chapter, "The Age of Elizabeth: The Beginnings of Journalism," Leavis discusses "the process by which the printing press came to supplement the human voice, and the conditions out of which journalism emerged" ("RJ," 7). He shows how journalism began with ballads and often came direct from the pulpit, yet, "[i]t was, of course, in the playhouse that Elizabethan England found completest expression" ("RJ," 7). The theater was a forum for the delivery of news as well as a cultural center. Not surprisingly, it was subject to attack, and Leavis quotes an exaggeratedly rhetorical passage from Stephen Gosson's "School of Abuse" (1579) attacking the theater. As Leavis notes, the Elizabethan period was "an age that seems to have been drunk with the newly realized power of language" ("RJ," 28). Indeed, as Dr. Johnson noted, *"The Trade of Writing"* ("RJ," 35) began in the Elizabethan period.

Throughout the opening chapter we see Leavis's interests in language and in cultural and social history interanimate each other. Despite the fact that there was life in the theater and the pulpit, direct journalistic commentary on current events was fraught with danger in an authoritarian society. The press was heavily censored. In 1599 John Stubbes and his printer had their right hands cut off for arguing against the Queen's anticipated French marriage, while Edmund Spenser employed allegory for safety in *The Faerie Queene* to get "'furthest from danger of envy and suspicion of present time . . . for avoiding of jealous opinions and misconstructions' " ("RJ," 45).

In the second chapter, Leavis examines the connection between journalism and the novel in the later seventeenth century. Although the journal ("diurnal") was born in 1622, Leavis argues that the second half of the seventeenth century saw the true birth of journalism, as well as significant developments in the relations between journalism and literature. For example, Leavis cites the case of Milton, who was censor of the press during 1651. Leavis's interest in the relation between journalism, literature, and life lead him to a perceptive assessment of the dynamic effect that Milton's political involvement had on the debate between the rebel angels in *Paradise Lost*.

Leavis discusses the advent of modern journalism in his third chapter, "Dryden, L'Estrange, and the Coffee-House." He argues that "the Coffee-houses were the nerve centres of London" ("RJ," 66). Later in the thesis he cites Leslie Stephen's *English Literature and Society in the Eighteenth Century* (1904), which notes that where there was 1 coffee-house in London in 1657, by 1708 there were 3,000. Leavis sees their proliferation and the reading of newsletters in them as instrumental in the development of modern journalism, although the theater continued to comment on current events. For example, John Dryden's prologues and epilogues are likened by Leavis to leading articles. Furthermore, he sees Dryden's *Absalom and Achitophel* (1681) as a superb example of the connection that had developed between journalism and literature, for he sees it as a "pamphlet in verse" ("RJ," 81).

In his fourth chapter, "The Growth of a Reading Public," Leavis shows how the complex society that had emerged at that time "needed the press" ("RJ," 141).He understands that a dynamic relationship must be established between the reading public and the journalist in order for a journal to thrive: "For a journal, unless it answers or awakens a certain demand, cannot live at all" ("RJ," 141). By 1809, 121 journals on the model of *The Spectator* had emerged. Leavis continues his discussion of the expansion of journalism in his Epilogue when he notes the advent of such newspapers as *The Morning Post* (1722) and *The Times* (1788) and the great quarterlies, the *Edinburgh Review* (1802) and the *Quarterly Review* (1809). The latter were of particular interest to the future editor of *Scrutiny* for they provided vehicles that allowed literary criticism to reach a wider audience than ever before. The great quarterlies, as *Scrutiny* later, "paid literature the tribute, and did it the service, of close and honest scrutiny" ("RJ," 332).

In discussing changes in literary style through the seventeenth century, Leavis notes the way in which Thomas Sprat's *History of the Royal Society* (1667) rejects "luxury and redundance of speech" and "all the amplifications and digressions of style" ("RJ," 90) that we find in Elizabethan writing in favor of "a close, naked, natural way of speaking, positive expressions, clear senses, a native easiness, bringing all things as near the mathematical plainness as they can,—and preferring the language of artisans, countrymen and merchants before that of wits and scholars" (qtd. in "RJ," 89). Sprat is describing what became the staple of Augustan prose style. As Leavis, with his intense interest in literary style, notes, the old complex, authoritarian style of Milton gives way to the new, plain style of Sir Roger L'Estrange. Though Milton's politics were Parliamentarian and L'Estrange's Royalist, Milton's prose style represented the old style of earlier seventeenth-century religious controversy, whereas L'Estrange's was the new style that anticipated the journalism of Joseph Addison and Richard Steele.

In the development of prose style, Leavis sees Andrew Marvell as an important transitional case. He "wrote with the coffee-house, not Milton or Clarendon in his ear" ("RJ," 98). Swift, Leavis argues, learned from Marvell's prose. But L'Estrange, as the most important journalist in England, had an influence on the development of English prose that, in Leavis's view, bears comparison with that of Dryden.

Arguing that a defining feature of journalism is its proximity to speech, Leavis credits journalism with the development, by the end of the century, of "a plain prose of general utility . . . workmanlike and supple, with everyday speech audible, as it were, behind it" ("RJ," 119). Leavis quotes Dr. Johnson: "Whoever wishes to attain an English style, familiar, but not coarse, elegant, but not catenatious, must give his days and nights to the volumes of Addison" ("RJ," 224). Furthermore, in his Epilogue, Leavis notes the colloquial style of the critics of the period of the emergence of the great quarterlies.

In his fifth chapter, Leavis discusses the importance of *The Tatler* and *The Spectator* in the development of the relationship between journalism and the novel. Of *The Tatler* he notes, "[t]he light, personal, intimate style gives it a life and a unity not to be found in any journal we have yet examined" ("RJ," 170). Steele himself, in *The Tatler,* No. 204, notes the close relationship between the prose of the journalist and common speech. Furthermore, Steele uses the term *novelist* to mean what we think of as a journalist—someone writing for a newspaper or journal. Leavis sees the connection between journalism and the rise of the novel in *The Spectator*'s "De Coverley" papers, which he sees as anticipating *Pickwick Papers* in its lively rendering of the "comedy of the London street" ("RJ," 208).

In Leavis's view, the early eighteenth century saw the press become increasingly important as a means of public communication. Steele, although he also wrote for the theater, helped the coffeehouse press to replace the theater as the most prominent source of journalism. *The Tatler* and *The Spectator* brought many of the attributes of the stage into the coffeehouse and transformed them for use in the novel. Thus, Leavis argues, in "*The Tatler* and the *Spectator* all the essentials of the novel [are] brought together except the unifying plot: character, action and dialogue, in a setting of town and country, fireside, street and tavern" ("RJ," 213).

In his sixth chapter, Leavis discusses the writing of Swift and Daniel Defoe. He believes that Swift could have been capable of writing "satirical novels of contemporary life" ("RJ," 247), but because of his involvement in the political controversies of his day, he "used authorship as the slave of ambition" ("RJ," 246). Leavis argues that the "fierce misery" apparent in Swift's work stems in part from a sense that his abilities were wasted. This, in turn, Leavis attributes to an "unsatisfactory relation . . . in his day between literature and life" ("RJ," 247). The reference to "fierce misery" indicates awareness of the self-hatred and consequent hatred of life in Swift that Leavis analyses so acutely in his later *Scrutiny* article "The Irony of Swift."

Leavis sees Defoe's style emerging from "the racy idiom of the street" ("RJ," 267), and his novels growing from his journalism as his "art blossoms out of the life of the community" ("RJ," 292). He argues that Defoe's business was to provide "the shopkeeper's wife with a theatre in which she could live the glittering life of the wicked, and yet, like Pamela, 'preserve her virtue,' nay more, reinforce it" ("RJ," 283). Defoe's case shows how journalism and the printing press help to transfer the attributes of the drama into the form of the novel, which can reach a burgeoning middle-class audience far beyond the physical range of the theater.

Leavis's seventh and final chapter concerns "The Booksellers," who replaced private patrons and came to control the publication and sale of books and magazines in the eighteenth century, men such as Robert Dodsley and Andrew Millar. He also considers the careers in literature of Henry Fielding, Johnson, Tobias Smollett and Oliver Goldsmith. Leavis notes that when the first three of these came to London, it was with the intention of writing for the theater. Fielding, indeed, wrote political journalism for the stage; his *The Historical Register* and *Pasquin* led to the Licensing Act of 1737. He turned to fiction when, because of censorship, it became impossible for him to continue to write for the stage. Leavis describes Fielding as born "to depict the world in which he lived" ("RJ," 302). Though noting "the heavy formalism of Johnson's style" ("RJ," 326), Leavis argues that "[i]n Johnson . . . Defoe and Swift were reconciled" ("RJ," 325). Noting the direct relationship between the letters of *The Citizen of the World* (1760) and the novel, *The Vicar of Wakefield* (1766), Leavis considers Goldsmith's style to have been formed by his work in journalism.

The Introduction to "The Relationship of Journalism to Literature" shows how Leavis himself liked to explore opposed positions in searching for a critically acceptable understanding. He begins his study by quoting Thomas Carlyle and George Bernard Shaw. Carlyle, according to Leslie Stephen, said that "Journalism is just ditchwater," while Shaw in 1908 argued that "Journalism can claim to be the highest form of literature, for all the highest literature is journalism" ("RJ," 1). For Leavis both statements were half-truths; he sought a different and fuller understanding. While it might be possible, by 1924, to agree with Carlyle that journalism had degenerated to "ditchwater," his comment was untrue of much earlier journalism that Leavis admired. Shaw, on the other hand, overstates his case. While Leavis shows throughout his thesis that great literature has the same relation to spoken language that we find in the best journalism, and that the novel, in fact, grew out of journalism, there is a difference in quality between great literature and journalism of which Shaw's comment shows no awareness. Leavis considers the movement in journalism that brought writing closer to speech one of the positive benefits of the relationship between journalism and literature. However, he argues that in contemporary society the press no longer has such a beneficial influence. Nevertheless, Leavis is optimistic that "[w]hatever the accompanying drawbacks may be now, the influence through which, when conditions were less complex, we clearly saw journalism serving literature, are still at work" ("RJ," 338). *Scrutiny* was an effort in vindication of this belief.

In 1930, Leavis published two pamphlets from his student Gordon Fraser's Minority Press: *Mass Civilisation and Minority Culture* and *D. H. Lawrence*. In the first, he argues the case for the importance of a minority doing its work in the face of the reduction of standards and the leveling-down process caused by mass civilization. Throughout his criticism,

Leavis writes from a perspective of perceived crisis, a stance inherited, perhaps, from Carlyle, John Ruskin, and Arnold. Leavis always stresses the urgency of his argument, the need for immediate application. He cites Oswald Spengler's *The Decline of the West* and H. G. Wells's *The Autocracy of Mr. Parham* as examples of contemporary awareness of the cultural crisis he is himself addressing. Leavis sees industrial technology as one of the chief causes of a breach in cultural continuity.

In support of this argument, Leavis draws on R. S. and H. M. Lloyd's *Middletown,* a study of a community in the American Midwest. This work discusses the changes wrought by the automobile, which has "in a few years, radically affected religion, broken up the family, and revolutionised social custom."[3] This process is not confined, in Leavis's view, to America, but is increasingly present throughout the Western world. He argues that this process of Americanization is widely acknowledged but not clearly understood. He is less concerned about the effects on community life of the material manifestation of mass production and standardization as represented by Woolworth's than he is about their effects in the field of mass communication represented by newspapers and film.

Like Q. D. Leavis in *Fiction and the Reading Public* (1932), Leavis sees the advent of Lord Northcliffe's *Daily Mail* as decisive and disastrous. His irony is clear: " 'Giving the public what it wants,' is clearly a modest way of putting it. Lord Northcliffe showed people what they wanted, and showed the Best People that they wanted the same as the rest" (*MCMC,* 19). Leavis is also highly critical of the cinema, another dominant feature of mass civilization. Films often effect, as Leavis puts it, "surrender, under conditions of hypnotic receptivity to the cheapest emotional appeals, appeals the more insidious because they are associated with a compellingly vivid illusion of actual life. It would be difficult to dispute that the result must be serious damage to the 'standard of living' " (*MCMC,* 22). Both newspapers and films, he implies, use applied psychology to manipulate their audience.

In the center of *Mass Civilisation and Minority Culture,* Leavis makes his intention in the work compellingly clear:

> Even those who would agree that there has been an overthrow of standards, that authority has disappeared, and that the currency has been debased and inflated, do not often seem to realise what the catastrophe portends. My aim is to bring this home, if possible, by means of a little concrete evidence. I hope, at any rate, to avert the charge of extravagant pessimism. (*MCMC,* 24)

Leavis sees Arnold Bennett as a living example of the degeneration of English literary culture. Bennett's "pontifical utterances from the *Evening Standard*" (*MCMC,* 26) are compared unfavorably with his pre–World War I articles in the *New Age.* For Leavis the problem with Bennett's self-assurance "is that there is no longer an informed and cultivated public. If there is no public to break into a roar of laughter when Mr. Bennett tells us that R. H. Mottram, like James Joyce, is a genius, or that D. H. Lawrence and R. H. Mottram (poor Mr. Mottram) are the two real British geniuses of the new age, how should there be a public to appreciate Mr. Bennett's modesty about poetry?" (*MCMC,* 29).

Here we come to one of Leavis's central critical concerns, the attempt to re-educate a public that will be able to judge the best of modern literature: the poetry of T. S. Eliot and the novels and stories of D. H. Lawrence. Besides the pronouncements of Arnold Bennett, Leavis also draws attention to those of J. C. Squire and Harold Munro: "Such pronouncements could be made only in an age in which there were no standards, no living tradition of poetry spread abroad, no discriminating public. It is the plight of culture generally that is exemplified here" (*MCMC,* 30).

Leavis believed that since the beginning of the nineteenth century the general ability to read with discrimination had deteriorated. It has become difficult for a serious critical journal to sustain itself:

> We ought not, then, to be surprised that now, when a strong current of criticism is needed as never before, there should hardly be in England a cultivated public large enough to support a serious critical organ. The *Criterion* carries on almost alone. It is accused of being solemn, and seems to owe its new-found security to a specific ecclesiastical interest. For the short-lived *Calendar of Modern Letters,* as intelligent and lively a review as ever appeared in English, died for lack of support. (*MCMC,* 31–32)

Nevertheless, within two years Leavis was editing *Scrutiny,* which he and Q. D. Leavis sustained for 21 years. Despite the small size of the "critically adult public" (*MCMC,* 32), the Leavises were able to raise the subscription list from 500 to 1,400 during their time with *Scrutiny.*

Leavis opens *Mass Civilisation and Minority Culture* with an epigraph from Arnold's *Culture and Anarchy* (1869) on the function of criticism: "And this function is particularly important in our modern world, on which the civilisation is, to a much greater degree than the civilisation of Greece and Rome, mechanical and external and tends constantly to become more so." Immediately noting the descent from the *Daily Tele-*

graph of Arnold's day to the *News of the World* of his own, Leavis argues
that the function of criticism could be more readily carried out in
Arnold's day than in 1930. Arguing for the importance of minority culture Leavis writes:

> In any period it is upon a very small minority that the discerning appre-
> ciation of art and literature depends: it is (apart from cases of the simple
> and familiar) only a few who are capable of unprompted, first-hand
> judgement. They are still a small minority, though a larger one, who are
> capable of endorsing such first-hand judgement by genuine response.
> The accepted valuations are a kind of paper currency based upon a very
> small proportion of gold. To the state of such a currency the possibilities
> of fine living at any time bear a close relation. There is no need to elabo-
> rate the metaphor. (*MCMC*, 14)

In support, Leavis cites I. A. Richards, *The Principles of Literary Criticism*
(1924):

> But it is not true that criticism is a luxury trade. . . . The critic, we have
> said, is as much concerned with the health of the mind as any doctor with
> the health of the body. To set up as a critic is to set up as a judge of val-
> ues. . . . For the arts are inevitably and quite apart from any intentions of
> the artist an appraisal of existence. Matthew Arnold, when he said that
> poetry is a criticism of life, was saying something so obvious that it is
> constantly overlooked. . . . He [the artist] is the point at which the
> growth of the mind shows itself. (*MCMC*, 14)

Leavis's reluctance to elaborate the monetary metaphor in the previous quotation together with his comment on the quotation from
Richards, "This last sentence gives the hint for another metaphor. The
minority capable not only of appreciating Dante, Shakespeare, Donne,
Baudelaire, Hardy (to take major instances) but of recognising their latest successors constitute the consciousness of the race (or of a branch of
it) at a given time" (*MCMC*, 14–15), should alert us to the importance
of considering the metaphoric life of Leavis's critical language.

Central to Leavis's concern throughout his criticism is the survival of
the best and finest uses of language, whether they be in criticism, fiction, or poetry. "For, as we noted above, when we used the metaphor of
'language' in defining culture we were using more than a metaphor. The
most important part of this 'language' is actually a matter of the use of
words. Without the living subtlety of the finest idiom (which is dependent upon use) the heritage dies" (*MCMC*, 44). To preserve "the finest

idiom" in the tradition of English literature is, then, Leavis's critical endeavor. Of course, it requires critical discrimination to identify this "finest idiom" both within the tradition and in contemporary writing. In *New Bearings in English Poetry* he analyses the contemporary situation in English poetry, then, in *Revaluation,* the post-Renaissance English poetic tradition as a whole. Throughout, Leavis is determined to be positive. Right to the end of his career he eschews pessimism:

> Are we then to listen to Spengler's and Mr. Henry Ford's admonition to cease bothering about the inevitable future? That is impossible. Ridiculous, priggish and presumptuous as it may be, if we care at all about the issues we cannot help believing that, for the immediate future, at any rate, we have some responsibility. We cannot help clinging to some such hope as Mr. Richards offers; to the belief (unwarranted, possibly) that what we value most matters too much to the race to be finally abandoned, and that the machine will yet be made a tool.
>
> It is for us to be as aware as possible of what is happening, and, if we can, to "keep open our communications with the future." (*MCMC,* 46)

Health, financial, and military metaphors are pervasive throughout Leavis's criticism. The metaphor of health expresses a search for both personal and cultural health. In analyzing the breach of continuity in English culture caused by such cataclysmic events as the French and industrial revolutions and World War I, Leavis argues that organic continuity has been violated. Nevertheless, he sought ways to heal this breach, to minister to an ailing culture. Financial metaphors, as in the quotation above, are connected with Leavis's preoccupation with value—spiritual as well as cultural, intellectual, and social values. Military metaphors appear to be prompted by Leavis's bitter experiences of World War I. The predominance of military metaphors throughout his critical writing suggests that Leavis saw life as a battle. He felt a duty as critic and teacher to fight the good fight on behalf of cultural values that he believed were under attack. Awareness of Leavis's metaphoric language adds a dimension to the present argument. Not only should we be aware of how Leavis connects close reading of texts with larger cultural and social issues but also be attentive to the underlying meanings of Leavis's own critical language. So, reading a sentence like the following, "Upon this minority depends our power of profiting by the finest human experience of the past; they keep alive the subtlest and most perishable parts of tradition" (*MCMC,* 15), should prompt us to consider its metaphoric dimension. Members of the minority culture offer us spiritual "profit," but they are also doctors or priests who minister to the body and spirit of a culture when "they keep alive the subtlest and most perishable parts of tradition." Leavis's sense of life is quite literally in his language, which requires of his reader the kind of careful attention that Leavis himself gives to poetry.

Leavis always argued that judgments of literature are judgments of life. He illustrates the relationship he saw between poetry and life with a quotation from I. A. Richards's *Practical Criticism* (1929):

> there is no such gulf between poetry and life as over-literary persons sometimes suppose. There is no gap between our everyday emotional life and the material of poetry. The verbal expression of this life, at its finest, is forced to use the technique of poetry; that is the only essential difference. We cannot avoid the material of poetry. If we do not live in consonance with good poetry, we must live in consonance with bad poetry. (qtd. in *MCMC*, 30)

Leavis's self-awareness in his use of language in critical discussion is quite evident when he writes that "[i]n their [the minority's] keeping, to use a metaphor that is a metonymy also and will bear a good deal of pondering, is the language, the changing idiom, upon which fine living depends, and without which distinction of spirit is thwarted. By 'culture' I mean the use of such a language" (*MCMC*, 15). Throughout his criticism, Leavis stresses the priority of language, the possession of which he sees as our defining human characteristic. Later, his principal argument against C. P. Snow is that the human world of language precedes the world of science that, in fact, emerges from it and without which it would be impossible, which is why there is one and not two cultures.

Though with the advent of Book Guilds and Book of the Month Clubs, Leavis saw "[s]tandardisation advanc[ing] to fresh triumphs" (*MCMC*, 36) and the term "high-brow" become "an ominous addition to the English language" (*MCMC*, 38), he determined to fight for the survival of "minority culture." Such a fight as Leavis fought for nearly 50 years required a clear-minded assessment of the situation before him. The following substantial passage in *Mass Civilisation and Minority Culture* supplies it:

> True: there were no "high-brows" in Shakespeare's time. It was possible for Shakespeare to write plays that were at once popular drama and poetry that could be appreciated only by an educated minority. *Hamlet*

appealed at a number of levels of response, from the highest downwards. The same is true of *Paradise Lost, Clarissa, Tom Jones, Don Juan, The Return of the Native.* The same is not true, Mr. George A. Birmingham might point out, of *The Waste Land, Hugh Selwyn Mauberley, Ulysses,* or *To the Lighthouse.* These works are read only by a very small specialised public and are beyond the reach of the vast majority of those who consider themselves educated. The age in which the finest creative talent tends to be employed in works of this kind is the age that has given currency to the term "high-brow." But it would be as true to say that the attitude implicit in "high-brow" causes this use of talent as the converse. The minority is being cut off as never before from the powers that rule the world; and as Mr. George A. Birmingham and his friends succeed in refining and standardising and conferring authority upon "the taste of the bathos implanted by nature in the literary judgments of man" (to use Matthew Arnold's phrase), they will make it more and more inevitable that work expressing the finest consciousness of the age should be so specialised as to be accessible only to the minority. "Civilisation" and "culture" are coming to be antithetical terms. (*MCMC,* 38–39)

In *Mass Civilisation and Minority Culture,* Leavis's exploration of language as a metaphor for culture permits him to unite the two interests I attempted to identify in his doctoral thesis: the concern with the relationship between literature and society and the concern with a close scrutiny of the language of literature.

With Shakespeare (and later Dickens), D. H. Lawrence is the writer who Leavis sees as uniting these concerns most completely in his creative work. Leavis's Minority Press pamphlet, *D. H. Lawrence,*[4] is the first, and most detached, of the three full-length discussions of Lawrence that Leavis undertook. With time, Leavis grew closer and closer to Lawrence seeing him, for example, as a much greater writer than T. S Eliot.

As early as 1930, though, Leavis regarded Lawrence as a genius. In ascribing genius to Lawrence, Leavis links him specifically with William Blake in a prophetic and visionary tradition in English writing. He quotes Lawrence from *Reflections on the Death of a Porcupine:* "In the seed of the dandelion, as it floats in its little umbrella of hairs, sits the Holy Ghost in tiny compass" (*DHL,* 4), and continues:

Passing from prophecy to squibs, one might point to *Pansies* and *Nettles,* which remind one of the similar verse in which Blake sought relief.

The community between Blake's and Lawrence's preoccupations is obvious: they might both be said to have been concerned with the vindication of impulse and spontaneity against "reason" and convention. The difference between them is the more interesting in that it is more than the difference between individuals. In the background of Blake are Rousseau and the French Revolution. In the background of Lawrence are the social transformations of the nineteenth century, Darwin, Dosto-evsky, Bergson, the War, and an age of psycho-analysis and anthropol-ogy. (*DHL*, 4)

At this stage of his criticism of Lawrence, Leavis regards *Sons and Lovers* (1913) as a novel in which Lawrence "is mature, in the sense of being completely himself" (*DHL*, 6). He values *The Rainbow* (1915) and *Women in Love* (1921) less highly in 1930 than he does in his 1955 *D. H. Lawrence: Novelist*. Leavis finds much of Lawrence's work uneven. While he admires *The Lost Girl* (1920), he finds *Kangaroo* (1923) a "disaster" (*DHL*, 19). However, Leavis was to continue to champion Lawrence's short stories and novellas; a remarkably large proportion of *D. H. Lawrence: Novelist* is devoted to discussing them. Leavis finds Lawrence's later novels, with the exception of *Lady Chatterley's Lover* (1928), charac-terized by "careless, hurried redundancy" (*DHL*, 20).

In spite of his admiration for its artistic maturity, Leavis presses a question that anticipates his later severe criticism of the novel: "And of *Lady Chatterley's Lover* we ask: If we accepted this, and all it implies, without reserves, what should we be surrendering? I had in discussion made my point with the random instance that we should be surrender-ing all that Jane Austen stands for" (*DHL*, 22). While Leavis values Austen much more highly than does Lawrence, he chooses not to answer in detail Lawrence's attack on Austen. He argues, however, that Lawrence's high valuation of "'the old blood-warmth of oneness and togetherness'" at the expense of "intelligence and the finer products of civilisation" (*DHL*, 25) can only lead to partial wisdom.

Leavis is perceptive about sex and religion in Lawrence: "There can hardly have been a sterner moralist about sex than Lawrence: it was for him the centre of a religion . . . That his religion was a reality to him there can be no doubt. But the reader is oppressed by the terrible monotony associated with it" (*DHL*, 15, 17). Also, Leavis is acute on Lawrence's preoccupation with "the dark God": "If the service of the dark God was the condition of Lawrence's magnificently sensuous vital-ity, and of his power to evoke strange modes of consciousness, then it is to that extent justified itself" (*DHL*, 17). However, "[i]t is plain that his devotion to the dark God is not so much an evangel of salvation as a symptom; a refuge from the general malady rather than a cure" (*DHL,* 18). Seeking moral and psychic health himself through the study of great literature, Leavis is sensitively aware of the nature of the same pre-occupation in Lawrence. He sees Lawrence's comments on Herman Melville as applicable to Lawrence himself: "And Melville really is a bit sententious; aware of himself, self-conscious, putting something over even himself. . . . He preaches and holds forth because he's not sure of himself. And he holds forth, often, so amateurishly" (qtd. in *DHL,* 20). Nevertheless, Leavis applauds E. M. Forster's obituary comment in the *Nation and Athenaeum* of March 29, 1930: "All that we can do . . . is to say straight out that he [Lawrence] was the greatest imaginative novel-ist of our generation" (*DHL,* 13).

In the closing pages of the pamphlet, summing up his sense of Lawrence's particular importance, Leavis endorses Spengler's account of the crisis in Western civilization brought on by industrialization: "the traditional ways of life have been destroyed by the machine, more and more does human life depart from the natural rhythms, the cultures have mingled, and the forms have dissolved into chaos, so that every-where the serious literature of the West betrays a sense of paralysing consciousness, of a lack of direction, of momentum, of dynamic axioms" (*DHL,* 28). Lawrence, he argues, represents part of the solution to that crisis for his "splendid human vitality, the creative faith, and the passion-ate sense of responsibility that make Spengler's fatalism look like an arduously mean exercise of self-importance" (*DHL,* 29). Lawrence's view is that if Western civilization collapses, "it must carry through all the collapse the living clue to the next civilisation" (qtd. in *DHL,* 30). This is Leavis's central thought. Lawrence's "living clue" becomes Leavis's "living principle." Increasingly we see Leavis carrying the torch of Lawrence's "fierce flame" (*DHL,* 24).

Throughout *Mass Civilisation and Minority Culture* and *D. H. Lawrence,* Leavis is critical of the lying language of advertising and its manipulative use of applied psychology. He quotes J. B. Watson's *The Ways of Behaviourism*: "My business experience has opened my eyes to how simply things can be put to the public—how in homely words nearly all the worthwhile truths of science can be set forth." (*DHL,* 31). In Leavis's view we must always be vigilant critics of language. For Leavis, Lawrence is right in his defense of language and civilization:

> Civilised life is certainly threatened with impoverishment by education based on crude and defective psychology, by standardisation at a low

level, and by the inculcation of a cheap and shallow emotional code. Lawrence's genius has done much to make this more widely and more keenly realised than before. It is a great service. (*DHL, 32*)

In his doctoral thesis and his two Minority Press pamphlets, Leavis laid a strong foundation for his future criticism. The culmination of the first phase of his criticism was the launching of *Scrutiny* and the publication in February 1932, by Chatto and Windus, of *New Bearings in English Poetry: A Study of the Contemporary Situation*. In his "Prefatory Note," Leavis indicates that *New Bearings in English Poetry* is not a survey of contemporary poetry but a discussion of the relationship of poetry to the modern world, as well as an argument in support of the modernist changes effected in English poetry, in particular by the work of T. S. Eliot. *New Bearings* was informed by the spirit of *The Calendar of Modern Letters* (1925–1927), which Leavis admired.

In *New Bearings,* Leavis argues that "[p]oetry tends in every age to confine itself by ideas of the essentially poetical," nevertheless, "[p]oetry matters because of the kind of poet who is more alive than other people, more alive in his own age."[5] Essentially, Leavis reintroduces and develops the argument from *Mass Civilisation and Minority Culture* that the poet is part of the minority that represents the finest intelligence of an age:

> He [the poet] knows what he feels and knows what he is interested in. He is a poet because his interest in his experience is not inseparable from his interest in words; because, that is, of his habit of seeking by the evocative use of words to sharpen his awareness of his ways of feeling, so making these communicable. And poetry can communicate the actual quality of experience with a subtlety and precision unapproachable by any other means. But if the poetry and the intelligence of the age lose touch with each other, poetry will cease to matter much, and the age will be lacking in finer awareness. (*NBEP,* 19–20)

Leavis describes his method in *New Bearings* immediately and clearly: "my main concern is with the concrete: to discuss critically what seems to me most significant in contemporary poetry, 'significance' being defined by the generalities I venture upon. I have endeavoured to confine myself as strictly as possible to literary criticism, and to remember that poetry is made of words" (*NBEP,* 11–12).

Leavis sees Victorian poetry perpetuated in the work of Edwardian and Georgian poets. For Leavis, the chief qualification for being a significant poet is "the essential one, the need to communicate something of his own" (*NBEP,* 17). Beyond that, "[a]ll that we can fairly ask of the poet is that he shall show himself to have been alive in our time. The evidence will be in the very texture of his poetry" (*NBEP,* 27). What Leavis looks for in the "texture of verse" in the modern period in which he lives and writes is "an unmistakable newness of tone, rhythm, and imagery . . . an utterly unfamiliar 'feel' " (*NBEP,* 27). For Leavis, "the only technique that matters is that which compels words to express an intensely personal way of feeling, so that the reader responds, not in a general way that he knows beforehand to be 'poetical,' but in a precise, particular way. . . . To invent techniques that shall be adequate to the ways of feeling, or modes of experience, of adult, sensitive moderns is difficult in the extreme" (*NBEP,* 28).

In *New Bearings,* Leavis considers how the crisis that he sees besetting English culture is manifested in the state of English poetry. The crisis in poetry, he argues, goes back almost fifty years and has its roots in the preconceptions about poetry inherited by the Victorians and Georgians from the great Romantics. Leavis challenges the idea, which he considers a definition of "the nineteenth century ideal of the poetical," that "the sublime and the pathetic are the two chief nerves of a genuine poesy" (*NBEP,* 15). This ideal, with its emphasis on arousing emotion rather than thought in the reader, saw no place for "wit, play of intellect, [and] stress of cerebral muscle" (*NBEP,* 16) in poetry. According to Leavis, nineteenth-century poetry "was characteristically preoccupied with the creation of a dream-world. Not all of the poetry, or all of the poets: but the preoccupation was characteristic" (*NBEP,* 17).

Though Leavis had not yet developed his idea that in the Victorian period the strength of the language in literature had gone into the novel, an idea linked with his work on the development of a public prose close to the spoken language, he already perceived the inadequacy of Victorian poetry to the Victorian age. He suggests that the Victorian poet's response to the alienation he feels from the world is not confrontation but withdrawal. Alfred Tennyson in "The Palace of Art" acknowledges the inadequacy of this response, but is unable to transcend it. Neither Robert Browning nor Matthew Arnold, in Leavis's judgment, is equal to the task. He does note Browning's use of "spoken idiom in verse," but does not discuss the use Browning or Tennyson made of the dramatic monologue, which Eliot and Pound adopted and adapted to the more inward interior monologue.

In the study's second chapter Leavis describes, "The Situation at the End of the First World War," precisely the point at which his own com-

mitment to English literature began. Thomas Hardy, W. B. Yeats, and
Walter De la Mare seemed to Leavis, then, to be the major poets. He
discusses Yeats's attempt to emerge from the Celtic twilight, part of the
escapist world of Victorian poetry, and quotes Yeats's remark in his *Auto-
biographies* that poetry had replaced religion for him: "I am very religious
and deprived by Huxley and Tyndall, whom I detested, of the simple-
minded religion of my childhood, I had made a new religion, almost an
infallible church of poetic tradition" (*NBEP,* 31). In spite of Yeats's dedication to an Irish renaissance and, particularly, a national theater, Leavis
argues that he was, at first, unable to break with the poetic tradition
that he inherited. Leavis notes a significant change in Yeats's poetry with
The Green Helmet (1912): "The new verse has no incantation, no dreamy,
hypnotic rhythm; it belongs to the actual, waking world, and is in the
idiom and movement of modern speech. It is spare, hard, and sinewy
and in tone sardonic, expressing the bitterness and disillusion of a man
who has struggled and been frustrated" (*NBEP,* 40). Leavis considers
that "the poetry of this later phase is a remarkable positive achievement:
Mr. Yeats was strong enough to force a triumph out of defeat" (*NBEP,*
42). The change Leavis observes in Yeats relates him to significant
changes that Leavis notes elsewhere in English poetry: "The verse, in its
rhythm and diction, recognizes the actual world, but holds against it an
ideal of aristocratic fineness. It is idiomatic, and has the run of free
speech, being at the same time proud, bare, and subtle. To pass from the
earlier verse to this is something like passing from Campion to Donne"
(*NBEP,* 42). Leavis believes that in his post-1912 poetry Yeats "has
achieved a difficult and delicate sincerity, and extraordinarily subtle
poise" (*NBEP,* 44). The difficulty that Yeats experienced in remaining in
touch with the finer consciousness of his age Leavis sees as a warning of
the difficulties confronting a poet attempting to transcend the Victorian
poetic inheritance.

Unlike Yeats, Leavis argues, Walter De la Mare was unable in his
poetry to confront the modern world. He sees De la Mare as a victim of
his own poetic spell, exploiting "the fairy tale stratum of experience"
(*NBEP,* 47). His is "a poetry of withdrawal, cultivating a special poetical
'reality'" (*NBEP,* 48) remote from poetry of the present world.

If, as Leavis suggests, De la Mare is "the belated last poet of the
Romantic tradition" (*NBEP,* 51), Hardy is a great, belated Victorian
poet—one whose "potential influence . . . did not impinge until it was
too late" (*NBEP,* 52). In discussing "The Voice," Leavis notes that the
poem "really does evoke the emptiness of utter loss, exhibiting that

purity of recognition which is Hardy's strength. His verse has no incantation: it does what it says, and presents barely the fact recognized by a mind more than commonly responsible and awake" (*NBEP,* 51–52). Hardy's greatness as a poet lies, for Leavis, "in the integrity with which he accepted the conclusion, enforced, he believed, by science, that nature is indifferent to human values, in the completeness of his recognition, and in the purity and adequacy of his response" (*NBEP,* 52–53). But Hardy is "a Victorian in his very pessimism, which implies positives and assurances that have vanished. He knows what he wants, what he values, and what he is" (*NBEP,* 52). These are certainties, Leavis implies, no longer possible in the modern world. "The simple pieties, the quiet rhythms, and the immemorial ritual of rustic life" (*NBEP,* 55), the bedrock upon which Hardy's poems stand, have vanished, and their absence defines the modern poetic environment.

Following his discussion of Yeats, De la Mare, and Hardy, Leavis turns his attention to the Georgian poetic situation. He argues that the popularity of Georgian poetry is a symptom of poor critical standards and the lack of an educated public. Leavis sees evidence of this in the frequent selection of Hardy's less significant poems and the omission of his great poems from anthologies of the period. He sees further evidence in the popularity of Rupert Brooke, John Masefield, and James Elroy Flecker.

Of the remaining poets of the Georgian movement, only J. C. Squire, Edmund Blunden, and Edward Thomas are singled out for individual attention. Squire is credited by Leavis with trying to overcome the "poetical," but his work merely focuses attention on "the bankruptcy of the tradition and the difficulty of a new start" (*NBEP,* 58). While Leavis regards Blunden as a poet of "genuine talent," he sees in his work an escapist longing for a green world "seen, not only through memories of childhood, but through poetry and art" (*NBEP,* 60). However, Leavis notes that "the stress behind the pastoral quiet becomes explicit in poems dealing with mental conflict, hallucination, and war experience" (*NBEP,* 59). Only Edward Thomas of the Georgian poets (in his case Leavis disputes the classification) is seen as a poet "of a distinctively modern sensibility" (*NBEP,* 61).

For Leavis, Blunden and Thomas appear to be watershed poets, Blunden representing the poetic past and Thomas the present. Leavis sees the "inevitability" in Thomas as "an exquisite economy" (*NBEP,* 61). Thomas's "exquisite particularity" (*NBEP,* 62) distinguishes his work from Georgian nature poetry. Exquisite economy and particularity are

qualities of Metaphysical poetry, and Leavis's description of a "characteristic poem" by Thomas could equally describe a poem by John Donne or
T. S. Eliot, which is to say that Leavis, in describing Thomas, is describing what he regards as modern poetry. So, a characteristic poem of
Thomas's "has the air of being a random jotting down of chance impressions and sensations, the record of a moment of relaxed and undirected
consciousness. The diction and movement are those of quiet, ruminative
speech. But the unobtrusive signs accumulate, and finally one is aware
that the outward scene is accessory to an inner theatre" (*NBEP,* 61).

Prior to discussing, in separate chapters, the work of three major
modern poets—T. S. Eliot, Ezra Pound, and Gerard Manley Hopkins—
Leavis makes a final survey of the modern and contemporary scene.
Thomas, like Wilfred Owen and Isaac Rosenberg whose work Leavis
admired, was killed during World War I. In any case, Leavis argues,
"even if they had been properly recognized at once, [they] could hardly
have constituted a challenge to the ruling poetic fashions" (*NBEP,* 64).
The Sitwells and Imagism are dismissed as serious opposition to the
Georgian movement, while the late laureate Robert Bridges's *The Testament of Beauty* Leavis finds "a disquisition in verse that is scholarly and
original, but dead" (*NBEP,* 65).

Leavis sees Eliot as the true originator of modern poetry. Pound's was
a secondary accomplishment, while Hopkins was an anticipator of the
inward way modern poetry would go. Eliot's *Poems 1909–1925* established modern poetry for Leavis. "The Love Song of J. Alfred Prufrock"
(1917), Leavis argues, overcomes the "poetical" tradition inherited from
the nineteenth century. It is "poetry that expresses freely a modern sensibility, the ways of feeling, the modes of experience, of one fully alive in
his own age" (*NBEP,* 67). Discussing "Portrait of a Lady," Leavis notes
Eliot's use of the "idiom and cadence of modern speech," the strictly disciplined "freedom and variety" of Eliot's verse, and the "audacities of
transition and psychological notation" (*NBEP,* 68) are evidence of Eliot's
originality and modernity.

Leavis admires the breadth and depth of reference in Eliot's work.
He argues that Eliot learned from French poetry, particularly from
Tristan Corbière and Jules Laforgue, a way forward not offered by
nineteenth-century English poetry. However, Eliot's understanding of
English literature, particularly his appreciation and use of Elizabethan
drama and the poetry of Donne, is also regarded by Leavis as important. For example, Leavis argues that "Gerontion" "expresses psychological subtleties and complexities in imagery of varied richness and

marvellously sure realization," and restores to English poetry "[q]uali-
ties that (if we ignore Hopkins as he was ignored) have been absent"
since that period (*NBEP,* 70).

In returning to this source, Eliot broke free from the Spenser-Milton-
Tennyson poetic tradition that Leavis sees as having led to the current
malaise in English poetry. He regards that poetic idiom, in its remoteness from spoken language, as making only partial use of "the resources
of the English language" (*NBEP,* 71), whose richness Eliot exploits fully.

In his discussion of *The Waste Land* we can see how Leavis once again
moves between close analysis and cultural criticism, as he reveals his
continuous interest in the relation between literature and culture.
Throughout *New Bearings,* Leavis argues that the Victorian poetic tradition, continued by the Georgian poets, is inadequate to confront the exigencies of an urban industrial society. Hardy, a late Victorian, still roots
his imagery in rural culture, while Eliot's imagery is urban. In considering *The Waste Land*, Leavis notes that "[t]he remoteness of the civilization celebrated in *The Waste Land* from the natural rhythms is brought
out, in ironical contrast, by the anthropological theme" *(NBEP,* 79). The
poem, he argues, is "an effort to focus an inclusive human consciousness" (*NBEP,* 81). Leavis's detailed analysis of *The Waste Land* does not
indicate unalloyed enthusiasm for the poem. He grants that many qualifications may be urged, not least of which is the charge that the poem is
only accessible to "an extremely limited public equipped with special
knowledge" (*NBEP,* 88). Leavis returns to his argument that this is a
symptom of the malaise in English culture. The most serious consequence of the situation is that in a "hostile and overwhelming environment" (*NBEP,* 88) only a limited artistic achievement is possible. In such
an environment, Leavis argues, "even Shakespeare could hardly have
been the 'universal' genius" (*NBEP,* 88). Leavis concludes, "when all
qualifications have been urged, *The Waste Land* remains a great positive
achievement, and one of the first importance for English poetry." Leavis
believes that Eliot, because of his intellectual brilliance and creative
originality, has solved problems for himself and in so doing has liberated
others. His work as poet and critic shows both the necessity of breaking
with the Victorian dreamworld and the way in which the break may be
made. In *The Waste Land,* Leavis argues, "a mind fully alive in the age
compels a poetic triumph out of the peculiar difficulties facing a poet in
the age"(*NBEP,* 95).

After analysis of *The Hollow Men,* the three *Ariel* poems ("Journey of
the Magi," "Song of Simeon," and "Marina"), and *Ash Wednesday,* Leavis

concludes his valuation of Eliot's importance by noting that "[t]he poetry of this last phase may lack the charged richness and the range of *Gerontion* and *The Waste Land*. But it is, perhaps, still more remarkable by reason of the strange and difficult regions of experience that it explores. . . . this poetry is more disconcertingly modern than *The Waste Land*" (*NBEP,* 109). Eliot, Leavis sees, as "more aware of the general plight than his contemporaries, and more articulate: he made himself (answering to our account of the important poet) the consciousness of his age, and he did this the more effectively in that he was a critic as well as a poet. (A like alliance of creation and criticism is to be found in Wordsworth and Coleridge; indeed we may expect to find them closely associated in any period in which tradition has failed the artist and needs to be radically revised.)" (*NBEP,* 158). Eliot, Leavis argues, establishes "new bearings in English poetry."

The other significant presences in modern English poetry, for Leavis, are Ezra Pound and Gerard Manley Hopkins. In the case of Pound, it is *Hugh Selwyn Mauberley* that Leavis regards as important. "In *Mauberley,*" he writes, "we feel a pressure of experience, an impulsion from deep within. The verse is extraordinarily subtle, and its subtlety is the subtlety of the sensibility that it expresses" (*NBEP,* 115). While he suggests that Eliot overestimates Pound's *Cantos* (Leavis refuses to separate form and content in the way that Eliot does), he argues that *Hugh Selwyn Mauberley* is an important poem that has "the impersonality of great poetry: his technical perfection means a complete detachment and control" (*NBEP,* 115).

Gerard Manley Hopkins is, for Leavis, a modern poet born before his time: "He is likely to prove, for our time and the future, the only influential poet of the Victorian age, and he seems to me the greatest" (*NBEP,* 156). Leavis regards him as "one of the most remarkable technical inventors who ever wrote, and . . . a major poet" (*NBEP,* 130). Detailed analysis of Hopkins's work, particularly "The Wreck of the *Deutschland*," "The Windhover," "Spelt from Sibyl's Leaves," and the Sonnets of Desolation lead Leavis to locate the strength of Hopkins's work, and its modernity, in the power of his imagery, the inner debate, and his ability to use "the living idiom . . . the speaking voice" (*NBEP,* 156). Unlike Charles Williams, who regarded Hopkins as a Miltonic poet, Leavis associates him with Shakespeare: "There is no essential characteristic of his technique of which it might not be said that it is a matter of 'using professedly' and 'making a principle' of something that may be found in Shakespeare" (*NBEP,* 137–38). What Hopkins offers the contemporary poet and reader, Leavis argues, is that "no one can come from studying his work without an extended notion of the resources of English. And a technique so much concerned with inner division, friction, and psychological complexities in general has a special bearing on the problems of contemporary poetry" (*NBEP,* 156). For Leavis, "Hopkins's genius was as much a matter of rare character, intelligence, and sincerity as of technical skill; indeed, in his great poetry the distinction disappears; the technical triumph is a triumph of the spirit" (*NBEP,* 148). "Technique" is a difficult term to define in Leavis's criticism, but it involves finding the means in language to express and communicate deeply and personally held meanings. Leavis is particularly interested in "inner division" as a sign of "sincerity" or "authenticity" in the "modern" poet. He prefers the Sonnets of Desolation to "The Wreck of the *Deutschland*" because, he argues, Hopkins's "skill is most unmistakably that of a great poet when it is at the service of a more immediately personal urgency, when it expresses not religious exaltation, but inner debate" (*NBEP,* 147). In the discussion of Eliot, Leavis suggests that *Ash Wednesday* is "an effort at resolving diverse compulsions, recognitions and needs," that it is about "self scrutiny, self exploration." The modern poet, he argues, can have "no pretence to Dante's certitude—to his firm possession of vision." In *New Bearings,* Leavis considers a poet "modern" when he confronts what he calls "adult distresses" (*NBEP,* 59)—characterized by the breach in continuity in English culture brought about by the industrial revolution and brought irresistibly to the attention of the contemporary poet by the cataclysm of World War I—in language close to "the living idiom" (*NBEP,* 152), rather than finding solace in the creation of a "dream world," which he sees as typical of Victorian and Georgian poetry. Eliot, Pound, and Hopkins "together represent a decisive reordering of the tradition of English poetry" (*NBEP,* 157). Eliot is the central figure: "Future English poetry (if English poetry is to continue) is likely to bear the same kind of relation to him as later Romantic poetry did to Wordsworth and Coleridge" (*NBEP,* 157).

In his final chapter, "Epilogue," Leavis reviews the contemporary situation in poetry. He sees William Empson's poems in *Cambridge Poetry 1929* as emerging naturally from the poetic reorientation that Eliot effected. Empson's poetry reveals a debt to Donne and to Eliot. Leavis argues that the effect of Eliot's criticism and poetry together "has been to establish the seventeenth century in its due place in the English tradition. In the seventeenth century (at any rate in the tradition deriving

from Donne) it was assumed that a poet should be a man of distinguished intelligence, and he was encouraged by the conventions to
bring into his poetry the varied interests of his life" (*NBEP,* 159–60).
Leavis sees Empson as answering to this description. Empson's "verse
always has a rich and strongly characteristic life, for he is as intensely
interested in his technique as in his ideas" (*NBEP,* 161).

The other contemporary poet who Leavis sees as important is Ronald
Bottrall. For Leavis, Bottrall is essentially a modern poet who has
learned "technically" from both Pound and Hopkins, but "[h]is world is
Mr. Eliot's; a world in which the traditions are bankrupt, the cultures
uprooted and withering, and the advance of civilization seems to mean
death to distinction of spirit and fineness of living" (*NBEP,* 165). Nevertheless, Leavis finds in Bottrall "a certain positive energy, an assurance
expressing itself at times that there is a course to steer, that bearings can
be found, that there is a possible readjustment to the conditions"
(*NBEP,* 166).

In Bottrall's poetry Leavis notes "how inseparably his command of
imagery is bound up with his command of rhythm" (*NBEP,* 169). In a
similar way, in Leavis's case, his close reading is inseparably bound up
with his interpretation of literature's relation to culture and society.
Leavis reads poetry to discover sincerity or its absence, a vital, personal
response to the human world or a dead and conventional one. Though
Leavis feels strongly positive about the poetic reorientation that Eliot,
Pound, and Hopkins effected and about the contemporary contributions of Empson and Bottrall, he is nevertheless concerned that
"[w]ithout a public poetry can hardly continue, and the ordinary cultivated reader is ceasing to read poetry at all" (*NBEP,* 170). Leavis fears
that there are no standards and no educated public. That Bridges's *The
Testament of Beauty* became a best seller, Leavis explains by suggesting
"that its sales show mainly with what success adroit journalism can
exploit even a vestigial habit" (*NBEP,* 170). In the face of modern dis-
continuity and the flood of contemporary print, the common reader has
"lost the education that in the past was provided by tradition and social
environment" (*NBEP,* 171).

Completing his account of "new bearings in English poetry," Leavis
reinvokes the argument already made in *Mass Civilisation and Minority
Culture.* In our time, poetry, literature, and art "are becoming more specialized: the process is implicit in the process of modern civilization"
(*NBEP,* 171–72). In the face of "standardization, mass-production, and
levelling-down," the "tiny minority" capable of "the highest level of

response" (*NBEP,* 172) must continue to do its work. Though "poetry in the future, if there is poetry, seems likely to matter even less to the world . . . Those who care about it can only go on caring" (*NBEP,* 172). Leavis cared. His literary, social, and cultural criticism from 1924 to 1932 reveal the depth and range of his concern.

Chapter Three
Revaluations: 1933–1936

Where *New Bearings in English Poetry* presents Leavis's account of the reorientation that had taken place in modern poetry, *Revaluation: Tradition and Development in English Poetry* (1936) provides his assessment of the post-Shakespearean English poetic tradition. Central to his argument is the idea already presented in *New Bearings* that if Donne, Pope, and Hopkins, rather than Milton and Tennyson, are seen as the natural successors to Shakespeare, a new understanding of the nature of poetic language and style follows; the language of English poetry is a dramatic language close to speech, that expresses vital realities, rather than a canorous language that affords escape into a dream world. However, in order fully to grasp the context of *Revaluation* and Leavis's development toward it, it is helpful to consider the works that preceded it: *How to Teach Reading: A Primer for Ezra Pound* (1932), *For Continuity* (1933), *Towards Standards of Criticism: Selections from "The Calendar of Modern Letters, 1925–1927"* (1933), *Culture and Environment: The Training of Critical Awareness* (1933), and *Determinations* (1934).

Leavis sees Pound's *How to Read* as offering a challenge. It asks important questions such as "What is the function of literary culture—its *raison d'être*? Why do we read, and why should we?"[1] Writing in the early 1930s, Leavis argues that there is now "no Common Reader: the tradition is dead ... Marxist communism is being much worn" (*HTTR,* 107). "It is plain, then, that if literary culture is to be saved it must be by conscious effort; by education carefully designed to meet the exigencies of the time—the lapse of tradition, the cultural chaos and the hostility of the environment" (*HTTR,* 107). This is as clear an expression as we have, at this time, of Leavis's belief in the importance of education. Only through education "carefully designed" can a minority capable of maintaining cultural standards be sustained. In an almost contemporary publication, *Towards Standards of Criticism* (1933), his introduction to a selection from *The Calendar of Modern Letters* (1925–1927), he defined literary criticism as providing "the test for life and concreteness; where it degenerates, the instruments of thought degenerate too, and thinking, released from the testing and energizing contact with the full living consciousness, is debilitated, and betrayed to the academic, the abstract and the verbal. It is of little use to discuss values if the sense of value in the concrete—the experience and perception of value—is absent."[2] For Leavis, an education in literary criticism, so understood, could sustain a minority capable of the finest consciousness of the age. Pound's importance is that he challenges us to think about such matters when he writes, "It appears to me quite tenable that the function of literature as a generated prize-worthy force is precisely that it does incite humanity to continue living; that it eases the mind of strain, and feeds it, I mean definitely as *nutrition of impulse*" (qtd. in *HTTR*, 108). Literature's function in the state, in Pound's view, "has to do with the clarity of 'any and every' thought and opinion. It has to do with maintaining the very cleanliness of the tools, the health of the very matter of thought itself" (qtd. in *HTTR*, 108).

Pound believes that "[g]reat literature is simply language charged with meaning to the utmost possible degree" (qtd. in *HTTR*, 110). While Leavis agrees with Pound about the value of literature to society, he questions Pound's local judgments, arguing that he displays "extravagant perversity" in excluding Shakespeare and Donne, including Theophile Gautier, and excluding Charles Baudelaire from his considerations (*HTTR*, 111). Leavis believes that Pound "exhibits in himself with rare and illuminating conspicuousness certain deficiencies that are a large part of the futility that he deplores in academic literary education" (*HTTR*, 112). For Leavis, there is a misconception involved in attempting to study technique apart from what is expressed through it. Developing this discussion, Leavis continues, "We have to speak of 'technique' as something distinct from 'sensibility,' but technique can be studied and judged only in terms of the sensibility it expresses. The 'technique' that is not studied as the expression of a given particular sensibility is an unprofitable abstraction, remote from any useful purpose of criticism" (*HTTR*, 113). Just as in *New Bearings in English Poetry* (114) Leavis argues against Eliot's willingness to separate form and content in his judgment of Pound, so here he argues against Pound's separation of "melopoeia" and imagery from meaning, because "imagery in poetry is not merely visual, still less a matter of seeing little pictures; it may correspond to all the sense that can be involved, and it may range from incipient suggestion so faint as not to be consciously registered to complete explicit realization" (*HTTR*, 115). "Poetic technique" and "critical sensibility" must, in Leavis's view, be trained together: "the cultivation of analysis that is not also a cultivation of the power of responding fully, delicately and with discriminating accuracy to the subtle and precise use of words is worthless"(*HTTR*, 116).

While Leavis admires the "vigour and directness" (*HTTR*, 118) of Pound's argument concerning the important function of literature in society having to do with "the health of the very matter of thought itself," he suggests that Pound has neither understood the relation of literature to language nor suggested its "relation to cultural tradition" (*HTTR*, 118). For Leavis, single works of literature cannot perform the function described by Pound unless they are part of a literary tradition. Leavis supports Eliot's argument from "Tradition and the Individual Talent" that " 'Mind' implies both consciousness and memory, and a literary tradition is both: it is the consciousness and memory of the people or the cultural tradition in which it has developed" (*HTTR*, 118–19).

In *How to Teach Reading* Leavis also considers the problem of prose. He suggests that criticism of prose requires the same kind of detailed analysis of language that he applies to poetry. While a critical technique appropriate to the analysis of prose may be difficult to develop and apply, Leavis sees it as possible and necessary. In a passage that contains the seeds of his idea of "the novel as dramatic poem" (to be more fully developed in *Towards Standards of Criticism*), he argues that "everything that the novelist does is done with words, here, here and here, and that he is to be judged an artist (if he is one) for the same kind of reason as the poet is" (*HTTR*, 125).

Leavis deplores education that teaches "the reverent approach to the masters" (*HTTR*, 127). He stresses both the indispensability of "literary history and knowledge of the background, social and intellectual" of literature, and the importance of the individual reading critically with an open mind. It is this combination, he argues, that should lead to an understanding of "the relation of the individual artist to others—to the contemporary world and the past," in other words of "what a literature is and what a tradition" (*HTTR*, 127).

In his scheme of work for the training of critical sensibility, Leavis recommends Eliot's essays "The Metaphysical Poets," "Andrew Marvell," and "John Dryden" published in 1921, as well as Sir Herbert Grierson's essays on the Metaphysical poets and the seventeenth century. The reader should compare these readings with his or her own analysis of Donne and Thomas Campion and of the relationship between the Metaphysical poets and Shakespeare, Thomas Middleton, Cyril Tourneur, and George Chapman. A comparison should be drawn between this work and the work of Milton. Further, the reader should explore the relationship between poetry and spoken language, the formation of poetic styles, the "line of wit" leading to Pope, and the influence of Milton on later poetic practice. This work, Leavis argues, should lead to an understanding of "the reconstitution of the English poetic tradition by the re-opening of communication with the seventeenth century of Shakespeare, Donne, Middleton, Tourneur and so on" (*HTTR*, 130), which has occurred in the twentieth century. However, an interest in tradition, Leavis argues, is only valid if tradition is understood in its relation to the present (*HTTR*, 130). As always, Leavis urges strongly that "no theoretical discussion should be allowed to go on for long at any distance from critical practice" (*HTTR*, 133).

Leavis believes that education in one's own language should have priority over education in other languages, including the classical languages. He quotes Wordsworth's *The Prelude*, Book VI, lines 105–14 to make this point:

> In fine,
> I was a better judge of thoughts than words,
> Misled in estimating words, not only
> By common inexperience of youth,
> But by the trade in classic niceties,
> The dangerous craft of culling term and phrase
> From languages that want the living voice
> To carry meaning to the natural heart;
> To tell us what is passion, what is truth,
> What reason, what simplicity and sense.
>
> (*HTTR*, 135)

Leavis's point is not that one should confine one's attention narrowly to one's own literature, but that one should, because of the inextricable link between literature and language, know one's own literature first. He argues that "if one is uneducated in one's own literature one cannot hope to acquire education in any serious sense by dabbling in, or by assiduously frequenting, any other" (*HTTR*, 134).

How to Teach Reading was published by the Minority Press in spring 1933. *For Continuity* followed in November.[3] In gathering periodical essays, *For Continuity* set a pattern for Leavis's later collections of essays: *The Common Pursuit* (1952);*"Anna Karenina" and Other Essays* (1967); and the posthumous collections edited by G. S. Singh, *The Critic As Anti-Philosopher* (1982) and *Valuation In Criticism and Other Essays* (1986). As well as reprinting the Minority Press pamphlets *Mass Civilisation and*

Minority Culture and *D. H. Lawrence, For Continuity* contained 10 articles and reviews from *Scrutiny* that Leavis had published since its inception a year earlier. He argues that the collection is more than the sum of its parts, for it makes a more powerful and unmistakable argument as a whole work whose parts "all illustrate, develop and enforce, in ways more and less obvious, the same preoccupation and the same argument—the preoccupation and the argument of *Mass Civilisation and Minority Culture*" (*FC*, 1). Leavis's interanimating preoccupations in *For Continuity* are with the quality of contemporary literature and its relationship to culture. Literature, for Leavis, is a cultural as well as a personal expression.

In *For Continuity,* Leavis considers such issues as " 'The Literary Mind' " and "What's Wrong with Criticism?"; the limitations of Theodore Dreiser; the importance of D. H. Lawrence in the face of T. S. Eliot's criticism; " 'This Poetical Renascence' "; and the limitations of James Joyce. The seventh essay in *For Continuity,* "John Dos Passos," provides a characteristic example of how Leavis's close reading works together with his cultural and social criticism. Leavis respects Dos Passos for engaging society honestly in his fiction, but he questions Dos Passos's belief in revolution as a foolproof social solvent.

One of Leavis's principle concerns in *For Continuity,* in the "Prefatory: Marxism and Cultural Continuity" and " 'Under Which King, Bezonian?' " is to criticize Marxism. As a result, Leavis remains a target for academic Marxists in the 1990s. He finds Marxism simplistic and unremittingly materialistic; for Leavis, it ignores the individual life. While he believes that some form of economic communism is inevitable *and* necessary (*FC*, 6), he detests the authoritarian and totalitarian forms that he saw Marxism, in practice, taking by the 1930s. In Leavis's view, Marxism in practice violates Marxist theory. Not everything, for Leavis, is definable in class terms. As he argues in his "Prefatory: Marxism and Cultural Continuity," "Cultural values—human ends—need more attention than they get in the doctrine, strategy and tactics of the Class War" (*FC*, 5). Leavis believes that "[t]here *is* . . . a point of view above classes; there *can* be intellectual, aesthetic and moral activity that is not merely an expression of class origin and economic circumstances; there *is* a 'human culture' to be aimed at that must be achieved by cultivating a certain autonomy of the human spirit" (*FC*, 9).

In " 'Under Which King, Bezonian?' " Leavis presciently notices what has, indeed, been the result of the twentieth-century's affair with Marxism *and* capitalism: "The essential differences are indeed now definable in economic terms, and to aim at solving the problems of civilisation in terms of 'the class war' is to aim, whether wittingly or not, at completing the work of capitalism and its products, the cheap car, the wireless and the cinema" (FC, 172). Television and the computer would come later.

In "The Literary Mind," Leavis defends literary culture against Max Eastman's championship of the scientific. He argues that while the tradition of literary culture is in a state of partial collapse, that there is "no centre and no authority" to which to appeal, literature, nevertheless, remains the discipline that must ask such central human questions as "what for? What ultimately for?" "Humane letters," Leavis suggests, "though they may have no authority in the province of 'certified facts,' have a good deal of authority in the question of what, in the long run, humanity is likely to find a satisfactory way of life" (FC, 63). This anticipates Leavis's argument with C. P. Snow by 30 years.

Leavis referred to *Culture and Environment: The Training of Critical Awareness,* which he wrote with Denys Thompson in about six weeks and which drew heavily upon Q. D. Leavis's work in *Fiction and the Reading Public,* as an "opuscule." This book was an attempt to disseminate the ideas of *Scrutiny* in the schools. Thompson, a former student of Leavis's, was by this time a schoolmaster.

Once more, Leavis, with Thompson, stresses the importance of education in attempting to re-establish cultural continuity that had been breached by industrialization. They emphasize, however, that education cannot replace what is lost, "the organic community with the living culture it embodied. Folk-songs, folk-dances, Cotswold cottages and handicraft products are signs and expressions of something more: an art of life, a way of living, ordered and patterned, involving social arts, codes of intercourse and a responsive adjustment, growing out of immemorial experience, to the natural environment and the rhythm of the year."[4] An understanding of that tradition must be brought to bear on our experience of the contemporary world. Again, Leavis argues that education is important because, "An awakening of consciousness will help people to become aware of the environment in which they live . . . Practical critical analysis of verse and prose can be extended to detecting falsity in advertising, journalism and popular fiction" (CE, 5–6).

Leavis and Thompson invite their university, Teachers' Training College, Workers' Educational Association (W. E. A.), Debating Society, study circle, and common readers to read Shakespeare and Bunyan's *Pilgrim's Progress* (1678–1684), "the supreme expression of the old English people . . . this great book, which is so much more than Bunyan's" (CE, 2), and George Sturt's *Change in the Village* (1912) and *The Wheelwright's Shop* (1923) in support of their argument. Industrial technology has effected a permanent change, they argue: "the advantage it brings us in mass-production has turned out to involve standardization and levelling-down outside the realm of mere material goods" (CE, 3). They quote *The Criterion*, volume 8, page 188 "The material prosperity of modern civilization depends upon inducing people to buy what they do not want, and to want what they should not buy" (CE, 26). They also present a number of examples of advertising copy for analysis in order to raise awareness of its exploitation of applied psychology. Students need to develop critical awareness of the possibilities of language and of the ways in which they can be exploited, through its manipulation, since "debasement of the language is not merely a matter of words; it is a debasement of emotional life, and of the quality of living" (CE, 48).

Leavis and Thompson quote an extended passage from D. H. Lawrence that shows how language works in the novel but also, by extension, how it works generally:

> It is the way our sympathy flows and recoils that really determines our lives. And here lies the vast importance of the novel, properly handled. It can inform and lead into new places the flow of our sympathetic consciousness, it can lead our sympathy away in recoil from things gone dead. Therefore the novel, properly handled, can reveal the most secret places of life. . . But the novel, like gossip, can also excite spurious sympathies and recoils, mechanical and deadening to the psyche. The novel can glorify the most corrupt feelings, so long as they are *conventionally* "pure." Then the novel, like gossip, becomes at last vicious, and, like gossip, all the more vicious because it is always ostensibly on the side of the angels. (qtd. in CE, 55–56)

Through George Sturt's *Change in the Village* and *The Wheelwright's Shop*, Leavis and Thompson consider "the old rural England" in which "speech was an art, as it still is in those parts of the country where the relics of the old culture still linger" (CE, 71–72). Leavis and Thompson note the importance of Sturt's refusal to use the term "hands" to describe his workmen, for they were "men and not 'labour,' not merely a factor necessary to production as 'power' and 'capital' are, and on the same level. Besides their hands, their brains, imagination, conscience, sense of beauty and fitness—their personalities—were engaged and satisfied" (CE, 75). No one in the enterprise was interested only in money.

The distinction Sturt makes is vital, Leavis and Thompson argue, because language is central to our culture: "Largely conveyed in language, there is our spiritual, moral and emotional tradition, which preserves the 'picked experience of ages' regarding the finer issues of life" (*CE,* 81). Since language is frequently "debased" by its use in advertising and journalism, Leavis and Thompson argue, it is important that knowledge of a literary tradition embodying the "finest" and "subtlest" use of language be kept alive (*CE,* 82). D. H. Lawrence, writing of the industrial Midlands, diagnoses the problem when he notes how "The industrial England blots out the agricultural England. One meaning blots out another. The new England blots out the old England. And the continuity is not organic, but mechanical" (qtd. in *CE,* 95). Though Leavis and Thompson admit that "we can't go back," nevertheless, "[i]t is important to insist on what has been lost lest it should be forgotten; for the memory of the old order must be the chief incitement towards a new, if ever we are to have one. If we forget the old order we shall not know what kind of thing to strive towards" (*CE,* 97).

In mid-twentieth-century England, education, for Leavis and Thompson, would necessarily be "*against* the [cultural] environment," though "[t]he aim of education should be to give command to the art of living" (*CE,* 106–7). They state that "[e]ducation demands energy, disinterestedness and a firm consciousness of function as never before" (*CE,* 109). They quote from J. MacMurray's *Learning to Live* that "[t]he main function of education is to train men and women for freedom, not for work . . ." (qtd. in *CE,* 145). *Culture and Environment* concludes with a bibliography in which the final item noted is *Scrutiny,* described as a "quarterly review, intended to keep those concerned about the drift of civilization (and especially those in schools) in touch with literature and the movement of ideas" (*CE,* 150). This description of *Scrutiny* makes it clear that Leavis is interested in literature in education as well as in its other cultural and social relations.

Introducing *Determinations* (1934), a selection of essays from *Scrutiny,* Leavis once again makes his central beliefs as a critic clear:

> Literary criticism, then, is concerned with more than literature. . . . A
> serious interest in literature cannot be merely literary; indeed, not only
> must the seriousness involve, it is likely to derive from, a perception of—
> which must be a preoccupation with—the problems of social equity and
> order and of cultural health. It is the modern disintegration that makes it
> urgent in our day to get a real literary criticism decisively functioning.[5]

The relation between close criticism of language and cultural criticism is implicit here.

By 1934 Leavis's critical direction was well established; he wrote in full confidence. He knew what he was doing and where he wanted to go. With hindsight we can see that *Revaluation* (1936) completes the first phase of his work on English poetry. *New Bearings in English Poetry* provides directions for analyzing the contemporary situation in poetry; *Revaluation* presents "new bearings" on the tradition of English poetry from Donne to Keats. Here Leavis undertakes the "scheme of work" described in *How to Teach Reading* (127–30). While *Revaluation* consists of independent essays, Leavis notes that it was conceived as a single work in conjunction with *New Bearings in English Poetry*. The two books are closely related. Leavis always emphasizes the necessity of understanding the relationship between the literary past and the present. In *How to Teach Reading* he asserts that "To initiate into the idea of living tradition except in relation to the present is hardly possible. An addiction to literature that does not go with an interest in the literature of to-day . . . goes with the academic idea of tradition—traditionalism, that is, in the bad sense" (*HTTR*, 130). In *Revaluation,* he argues that "[a]n account of the present of poetry, to be worth anything, must be from a clearly realized point of view, and such a point of view, if it is critically responsible, must have been determined and defined as much in relation to the past as to the present."[6]

Revaluation, then, is written to show "the essential structure" (*R,* 10) of the development of English poetry from Donne to Keats. It completes the brief account given of this development in *New Bearings.* In presenting his discussion of this development, Leavis acknowledges his debt as a "teacher" to his students. Since what criticism undertakes is "the profitable discussion of literature" (*R,* 14), Leavis notes "if I learnt anything about the methods of profitable discussion I have learnt it in collaboration with them" (*R,* 15). In chapter 1, "The Line of Wit," Leavis argues that Eliot has helped to establish the modern acceptance of Donne. We again read Donne as a "living poet." His "utterance, movement, and intonation are those of the talking voice" (*R,* 18). There is a vital drama of debate in Donne's poetry, "the technique, the spirit in which the sinew and living nerve of English are used—suggests an appropriate development of impressions that his ear might have recorded in the theatre" (*R,* 19). Leavis's metaphor of the vital body shows how much he cherishes the life of a poet's language. He speaks too of "Jonson's rooted and racy English" (*R,* 23). "The Line of Wit"

that Leavis sees in seventeenth-century poetry is a living line: "The line
. . . runs from Ben Jonson (and Donne) through Carew and Marvell to
Pope" (R, 32). It is the line of vital, dramatic Shakespearean English,
not the Latinate line that runs from Spenser through Milton and the
eighteenth-century Miltonists to Tennyson.

In chapter 2, "Milton's Verse," Leavis shows the distance from spoken
language and the externality of Milton's Grand Style. Milton, in Leavis's
view, writes English as if it were Latin, "cultivating so complete and sys-
tematic a callousness to the intrinsic nature of English, Milton forfeits
all possibility of subtle or delicate life in his verse" (R, 50). Leavis argues
that, after Comus, Milton loses "all feeling for his native English" (R, 51).
To indicate what he means by the Shakespearean as opposed to the Miltonic use of English, Leavis quotes a passage from Donne's Satire III:

> On a huge hill,
> Cragged and steep, Truth stands, and hee that will
> Reach her, about must, and about must goe;
> And what the hills suddeness resists, winne so;
> Yet strive so, that before age, deaths twilight,
> Thy Soule rest, for none can wake in that night.
>
> (R, 52)

Leavis comments, "This is the Shakespearean use of English; one might
say that it is the English use—the use, in the essential spirit of the language, of its characteristic resources" (R, 52). In contrast, "Tennyson
descends from Spenser by way of Milton and Keats, and it was not for
nothing that Milton, to the puzzlement of some critics, named Spenser
as his 'original'" (R, 53). Of Lycidas, Leavis writes, "The consummate
art of Lycidas, personal as it is, exhibits a use of language in the spirit
of Spenser—incantatory, remote from speech" (R, 53). For Leavis, Milton's poetry shows "character" rather than "intelligence," and is often
mechanical (R, 56).

Leavis's third chapter concerns Pope who, he believes, reveals a wit
that "comprehended not only the audacities of Donne, but also the
urbane critical poise of Ben Jonson" (R, 66). Leavis argues that "[w]hen
Pope contemplates the bases and essential conditions of Augustan culture his imagination fires to a creative glow that produces what is poetry
even by Romantic standards. His contemplation is religious in its seriousness" (R, 73). For Leavis, the fourth book of The Dunciad (1743) is
Pope's greatest achievement, and one that demonstrates irrefutably
"that satire can be great poetry" (R, 80). Besides, "Pope's puns are rarely

mere puns; they appear to be a distinctly personal and period development out of the metaphysical conceit: by them 'the most heterogeneous ideas are yoked by violence together'—the most diverse feelings and associations are brought into co-presence" (*R,* 86).

In the central chapter of *Revaluation,* "The Augustan Tradition and the Eighteenth Century," Leavis argues that in spite of the "fertile, varied and influential" example of Pope, who with Johnson, Goldsmith, and George Crabbe, represents the strength of the century, "the prevailing modes and conventions of the eighteenth century did not . . . bring into poetry the vitality of the age" (*R,* 87). In Leavis's view, the social and economic changes in English society following the Civil War spurred changes in intellectual and literary fashions. It was an age, he argues, in which "[g]ood form was in intimate touch with the most serious cultural code" (*R,* 96). While Leavis acknowledges that the concern with "manners" and "correctness" has an underlying serious moral concern, he argues that only a great poet could write profound poetry within the conventions and idioms dictated by the code of "good form." Pope, whose most "profound poetry has in it an essential element of the Metaphysical" was, in Leavis's view, such a poet—"a genius, both belonging to his time and transcending it" (*R,* 95).

Finding the difficulties of writing profound poetry in such a cultural environment insurmountable, lesser talents, Leavis argues, followed a "by-line" derived by Pope from the "minor poems of Milton" (*R,* 88). Here, Leavis detects "the co-presence of two distinct and ill assorted styles," one epitomized by "the neat and sedate . . . elegiac mode of Gray" (*R,* 88), the other by "Thomson's declamatory Miltonics" (*R,* 90). This "by-line," Leavis asserts, is "literary and conventional in the worst sense of those terms" (*R,* 90). If, as Leavis suggests, this line came to be seen as the main line of eighteenth-century poetry, it is because Pope, alone, represented the strength of the tradition Leavis regards as major. As always, Leavis's judgments arise from close analysis of individual works. So, while he deplores the verse that "keeps its monotonous tenor along the cool sequestered vale of Polite Letters" (*R,* 90), he acknowledges the success of Thomas Gray's *Elegy,* in which "his commonplaces are weighted by the idiom of a literary culture that laid peculiar stress on the normally and centrally human as manifested on the common-sense social surface of life" (*R,* 91).

Leavis believes that Wordsworth's poetry, like Pope's, represents "the full vitality of the age"(*R,* 97). But how do we get from Pope to Wordsworth? What elements do they have in common? What changes occur between them? The spoken idiom that Leavis cherishes is clearly something that Pope and Wordsworth share, though its style has changed from a vital polite to a vital common speech. Johnson is the poet who comes between them, more literary and less social than Pope, "[i]nhabiting as a writer the study, the library, or the garret" (R, 98). Nevertheless, Johnson's "literary" sense "was inseparable from a profound moral sense in the ordinary meaning of 'morality' " (R, 99). This is what comes down to Wordsworth who, like Pope and Johnson, has a profound, and profoundly animating, moral concern, what Leavis identifies in all three poets as "human centrality" (R, 99).

As usual, Leavis's analysis is detailed and delicate. Of Johnson's line, " 'For such the steady Romans shook the world' " he comments: "—That 'steady' turns the vague cliché, 'shook the world,' into the felt percussion of tramping legions" (R, 100). As I argue throughout, Leavis's discussions of the effect of cultural-social change on literary style grow naturally from his sensitive awareness of language, its changes and development.

In his discussion of the movement from Augustan to Romantic poetry, Leavis considers the case of Blake: "his genius was that he saw no choice but to work out a completely and uncompromisingly individual idiom and technique" (R, 104). Leavis sees Blake as offering "an extreme contrast with Burns, whose importance for the English tradition is that, while exemplifying a complete freedom from the English literary modes of the century . . . could be an influence at once in English poetry—he clearly counts for much in the emancipation represented by the *Lyrical Ballads*" (R, 104). Clearly, the change in sensibility and style from Pope to Wordsworth was effected, in part, by such alterations in taste as embracing ballad and other forms of popular poetry, such as the hymn. Perceptively aware of the complexity of changes in style and sensibility, Leavis notes the "peculiarly eighteenth-century strength" of Crabbe who has, Leavis believes, the strength of "a novelist and of an eighteenth-century poet who is positively in sympathy with the Augustan tradition" (R, 105). However, Leavis argues that Crabbe belonged to an older order; "the fine point of consciousness in his time" finds expression in the "congenial idioms and forms of Wordsworth and Coleridge" (R, 108).

Leavis completes his discussion of "The Augustan Tradition and the Eighteenth Century" with nine supporting notes. In these he presents a number of supplementary points and quotations. In commenting on William Collins's relation to Milton, he makes the point that "reminiscence and unconscious reminiscence" is what "inspiration so often turns out to be" (*R*, 111). Wordsworth, on the other hand, differs from Mark Akenside and Walter Savage Landor in having "new life to offer" (*R*, 113). Leavis, as always, stresses the personal element, the importance of having something of one's own to say. For example, commenting on Matthew Green's *The Spleen* (1737), he writes, "Green, in his Horatianism, is a good positive Augustan (he is a more engaging poet than Swift), exhibiting the strength of the age in what is at the same time a personal quality" (*R*, 115). Leavis notes, too, the differences between Pope's and Byron's spoken idiom: "Byron speaks as a man of the world and a gentleman, but not only is he not polite, the very essence of his manner is a contemptuous defiance of decorum and propriety. Irreverence about religion is something we cannot imagine in Pope" (*R*, 126). Further, Leavis remarks that "Byron the satirist has less affinity with Pope than with Burns" (*R*, 127). He concludes, "It is not for nothing, then, that the poet who ends the line of great satirists that started with Dryden belongs to the Regency, in which the eighteenth century ends. The eighteenth-century element in him is essential to his success, and yet has at the same time the effect of bringing out how completely the Augustan order has disintegrated" (*R*, 129).

The final three chapters of *Revaluation* concern Wordsworth, Shelley, and Keats. As noted in the opening chapter of the present study, Leavis had a strong affinity with Wordsworth. In *Revaluation*, Leavis felt a need "to revalue Wordsworth, to achieve a clearer insight and a fresh realization" (*R*, 130). Against Coleridge, Leavis shares Arnold's view that Wordsworth's "philosophy" is an "illusion" (*R*, 130–31). Leavis argues that while Book II of *The Prelude*, for example, appears to have an argument that could be paraphrased, it is impossible to paraphrase (*R*, 131). However, while Wordsworth's "philosophizing" is found wanting, Leavis sees it as an "expression of his intense moral seriousness and a mode of the essential discipline of contemplation that gave consistency and stability to his experience" (*R*, 137). Leavis argues that Wordsworth had, not philosophy, but wisdom to offer, that "the poetry . . . is complete and satisfactory; it defines convincingly . . . the sense of 'belonging' in the universe, of a kinship known inwardly through the springs of life and consciousness and outwardly in an interplay of recognition and response" (*R*, 136). For Leavis, Wordsworth was more than a "nature" poet, for Wordsworth's central focus is "the Mind of Man— / My haunt, and the main region of my song" (qtd. in *R*, 139). Wordsworth's interest in "ultimate sanctions" and "the living connexions between man and the extra-human universe" (*R*, 139) is, like Lawrence's, religious.

In *Revaluation*, Leavis finds Wordsworth's poetry directly helpful in facing the sickness of the twentieth-century, because he can make us aware of the possibility in human life of "a distinctly human naturalness; one . . . consummating a discipline, moral and other" (*R*, 142). This, surely, is what is meant by Wordsworth as a "poet of Nature," in effect, a poet of human nature. But if human nature is his first concern, it is clear that Wordsworth "drew strength from his sense of communion with the non-human universe" (*R*, 146). Quoting the description of the Wanderer from the first book of *The Excursion*, Leavis sees it as describing how Wordsworth himself would like to have been. However, unlike the Wanderer, "Wordsworth's course had not been steady; he sought the Wanderer's 'equipoise' just because of the 'piteous revolutions' and 'the wild varieties of joy and grief' that he had so disturbingly known. The Wanderer could not have written Wordsworth's poetry; it emerges out of Wordsworth's urgent personal problem; it is the answer to the question: 'How, in a world that has shown itself to be like this, is it possible to go on living?' " (*R*, 148). Leavis, during and following his experience of World War I, must have asked himself this question many times. "Behind, then, the impersonality of Wordsworth's wisdom there is an immediately personal urgency" (*R*, 148). The same is true of Leavis's literary criticism; he distinguishes between a "personal" and a "selfish" concern, and, in doing so, poses a question as urgent for himself following World War I as for Wordsworth following the French Revolution: "For if his problem was personal, it was not selfishly so, not merely self-regarding; and it is also a general one: if (and how shall they not?) the sensitive and imaginative freely let their 'hearts lie open' to the suffering of the world, how are they to retain any health or faith for living? Conflicting duties seem to be imposed (for it is no mere blind instinct of self-preservation that is in question). Wordsworth is not one of the few great tragic artists, but probably not many readers will care to censure him for weakness or cowardice" (*R*, 149). Because of his own experiences of World War I, Leavis was peculiarly able to sympathize with what Wordsworth had undergone in France. Personal feeling, sympathetic and general understanding are movingly present in the sentence, "A disciplined limiting of contemplation to the endurable, and, consequently, a withdrawal to a reassuring environment, became terrible necessities for him" (*R*, 149).

As Leavis came to consider the nature of tragedy, Wordsworth was important in his thinking. With Leavis's help, it is possible to see connections between Wordsworth's *The Ruined Cottage,* Isaac Rosenberg's "Dead Man's Dump," and Shakespearean tragedy. Leavis writes of *Margaret; or, The Ruined Cottage,* "It is significant that (whatever reason Wordsworth may have had for putting it there) the story of Margaret should also, following, as it does, close upon the description of the Wanderer, appear in Book I of *The Excursion.* It seems to me the finest thing that Wordsworth wrote, and it is certainly the most disturbingly poignant" (*R,* 149). As Wordsworth passes from *The Ruined Cottage,* begun in 1797 and completed by 1798, to *Michael,* written in 1800, and *Ode to Duty,* written in 1805, Leavis sees an increase in detachment and distance. In Wordsworth's movement to the public platform and the public voice, Leavis sees a loss of the balance and sensitivity that he associates with the inner voice that informs Wordsworth's best work. Even the *Immortality Ode,* Leavis suggests, although containing "decided elements of the living," is tainted by a foretaste of the formality that he finds deadening in Wordsworth's public voice. In *The Prelude* (1850), Leavis argues, "in the pursuit of formal orthodoxy" Wordsworth "freely falsified and blunted the record of experience" (*R,* 153).

Late in his life, Leavis returned to his preoccupation with Wordsworth. He described his 1970 essay, "Wordsworth: The Creative Conditions" as "the best thing I've done" (MacKillop, 19), and his last published notes are on Wordsworth. Writing 34 years after *Revaluation,* Leavis asserts that "[g]reat literature has its life in the present, or not at all" ("Wordsworth," 24). This being the case, it follows that any writer worthy to be called great must be seen to have value for the contemporary reader. Leavis vehemently opposes the "inert concurrence in conventional valuations and reputations" ("Wordsworth," 24), implying that valuation and revaluation must be carried on continuously. This is the process Leavis attempts to follow in his critical practice when he analyses Wordsworth's poetry. He tries to locate the "great" Wordsworth, to define its "innovating power, its importance and the nature of his [Wordsworth's] originality" ("Wordsworth," 25). Just as Leavis sees a parallel between Pope's contemporaries and successors in the eighteenth century and the Georgian poets of the early twentieth century, so too he sees a parallel between what Wordsworth achieved at the end of the eighteenth century and what Eliot achieved around 1918. Both poets, he argues, "altered expression."[7] Wordsworth, important in his own right, also provided an important example for Shelley and Keats, for his "success in expressing creatively and intensely a profoundly individual sensibility gave later contemporary poets the impulsion they needed" ("Wordsworth," 27). Leavis cites Shelley's "Peter Bell the Third" in support of this argument, for Shelley shows how Wordsworth's "individual mind" and language was of decisive importance to practitioners like Keats and himself ("Wordsworth," 25–30).

As in *Revaluation,* Leavis sees "The Ruined Cottage" (1797–1798) as a poem of central importance in Wordsworth's development, for it is here that Wordsworth's "alteration of expression" takes place ("Wordsworth," 37). Wordsworth manages to hold a "tense and difficult poise" ("Wordsworth," 38) "between the two personae" of the Wanderer and himself the poet ("Wordsworth," 39). Here, Wordsworth's style "accommodates readily and naturally the representation of natural speech" ("Wordsworth," 34), an attribute that Leavis characteristically prefers to "conventional poetizing" (*R,* 88). In his best work, Leavis suggests, Wordsworth's English, "in its naturalness and flexibility," owes a debt to Shakespeare not to Dryden or Milton ("Notes," 299). It is a style able to register the human tragedy of the poem with "heart-piercing immediacy" ("Wordsworth," 34). Here we should recall the profound impact that the French Revolution had upon Wordsworth. As a great poet, Wordsworth gave voice to what he experienced: "He witnessed, close at hand, hopes frustrated, suffering entailed upon the innocent and helpless, and diverse kinds of human deterioration, he being very young" ("Wordsworth," 37). As in *Revaluation,* however, Leavis notes, that the "equipoise" Wordsworth achieves in "The Ruined Cottage" "settles into security (and security, remember, is on the way to inertness)" ("Wordsworth," 40). Once Wordsworth's creativity lapsed into habit "or the Wanderer's philosophic calm, it had lost its intransigence. It had lost, that is, its creativity" ("Wordsworth," 40).

Nevertheless, for Leavis, Wordsworth's example shows "creative genius pushing forward the frontiers of language and in the perception which is thought achiev[ing] the new"("Notes," 299). In his discussion of Wordsworth, Leavis suggests that in studying great poetry "we advance our knowledge of ourselves" ("Notes," 299), because a great poem is "a coherent act of expression capable of carrying the reader into the realm of 'knowledge' and 'being' the poet entered with that act of creation" ("Notes," 299). Further, Leavis argues that an attempt to understand Wordsworth should lead to intelligent thought about "meaning, value and art-speech," and about the very nature of life ("Notes," 300). This is why Leavis regards Wordsworth as a great poet with particular relevance to "our present sick civilization" ("Notes," 298). These are Leavis's latest thoughts on Wordsworth. His attempt to define the nature of Wordsworth's greatness, begun in *Revaluation* and continued into "Wordsworth: the Creative Conditions" and his late notes, is one of the most important endeavors in his criticism, as important (though less recognized) as his life-long engagements with Eliot and Lawrence. Though Leavis succeeded, in large measure, in defining the nature of Wordsworth's poetic achievement, he thought that Wordsworth was undervalued and deserved still more critical attention. Leavis did not live to complete his work on Wordsworth to his own satisfaction.

In the penultimate chapter of *Revaluation,* Leavis discusses Shelley. He responds to Eliot's comments on finding Shelley intoxicating at 15 and unreadable in maturity (*R,* 170). When he considers "Shelley's . . . characteristic modes of expression" (*R,* 171), Leavis is troubled by the frequent vagueness of Shelley's language and "his weak grasp upon the actual" (*R,* 172). Close analysis of "Ode to the West Wind" causes Leavis to note a "general tendency of the images to forget the status of the metaphor or simile that introduced them and to assume an autonomy and right to propagate, so that we lose in confused generalizations and perspectives the perception or thought that was the ostensible *raison d'être* of imagery" (*R,* 172). Shelley's poetry, known for its emotion and lyricism, is successful, Leavis suggests, only if the reader responds to it emotionally without bringing critical intelligence to bear upon the poem (*R,* 173). Leavis argues that "Shelley at his best and his worst, offers the emotion itself, unattached, in the void," while his "inspiration" sometimes becomes "poetical" habit (*R,* 178). In this connection, Leavis notes Shelley's frequent use of such words as *"radiant, aërial, odorous, daedal, faint, sweet, bright, winged, -inwoven"* as well as *"charnel, corpse, phantom, liberticide, aghast,* [and] *ghastly"* (*R,* 179). These Leavis calls "fondled vocabulary" (*R,* 179). Shelley, Leavis argues, belongs in the line running through Spenser and Milton to Tennyson. There is a particular affinity, he suggests, between Shelley and Algernon Swinburne (*R,* 192).

Leavis takes issue with Shelley's theory of inspiration and poetic composition presented in his *Defense of Poetry.* Shelley's overriding emphasis on spontaneity as a value leads, Leavis argues, to the position that "'Inspiration' is not something to be tested, clarified, defined, and developed in composition" (*R,* 175). Nevertheless, Leavis notes the importance of what he sees as Shelley's unfortunate poetic theory and practice on the "later notion of the 'poetical'" (*R,* 191). Leavis deplores the rejection of intellectual discipline that he sees as inherent in Shelley's position. He contrasts it with Wordsworth's "recollection in tranquil-

lity," which, he argues, suggests a process of "emotional discipline, critical exploration of experience, pondered valuation, and maturing reflec-
tion. As a result of it an organization is engaged in Wordsworth's poetry,
and the activity and standards of critical intelligence are implicit"
(R, 176).

Nevertheless, Leavis sees Shelley as, at times, "unmistakably a distinguished poet" (R, 176). In spite of the severe limitations he sees in "Ode
to the West Wind," Leavis notes that "the consummate expression is
rightly treasured" (R, 190). *The Mask of Anarchy* is singled out by Leavis
for its "rare emotional integrity and force, deriving from a clear, disinterested, and mature vision" (R, 189). The poem contains an "unusual
purity and strength . . . there is nothing of the usual Shelleyan emotion-
alism—no suspicion of indulgence, insistence, corrupt will, or improper
approach. The emotion seems to inhere in the vision communicated, the
situation grasped: Shelley sees what is in front of him too clearly, and
with too pure a pity and indignation, to have any regard for his emo-
tions as such; the emotional value of what is presented asserts itself, or
rather, does not need asserting. Had he used and developed his genius in
the spirit of *The Mask of Anarchy* he would have been a much greater,
and a more readable poet" (R, 190). Leavis's chapter on Shelley in *Revaluation* is one of his most memorable, stringent in its adverse commentary on Shelley's limitations but generous in its recognition of the strong
places in Shelley's work. Taken as a whole it is excellent literary criticism, critical in the best sense.

In the final chapter of *Revaluation,* Leavis discusses Keats's poetry. He
affirms the "current placing" of Keats but suggests that his work
deserves "sharper" analysis (R, 199). Such analysis of "Ode to a Nightingale" shows, Leavis argues, that Keats is more than an exponent of "art
for art's sake" (R, 201). Unlike A. C. Bradley, Leavis sees "Ode to a
Nightingale" as a much better poem than Shelley's "To a Skylark." In
Keats's ode, Leavis finds that "The rich local concreteness is the local
manifestation of an inclusive sureness of grasp in the whole . . . when we
re-read it we find that it moves outwards and upwards towards life as
strongly as it moves downwards towards extinction; the *Ode* is, in fact,
an extremely subtle and varied interplay of motions, directed now positively, now negatively" (R, 202).

In discussing "Ode on a Grecian Urn," Leavis shows Keats's relationship to "[t]he Pre-Raphaelite cult of Beauty, which developed into the
religion of Art (or the aesthetic religiosity) . . . the completest expression
of . . . Victorian romanticism" (R, 210). But, Leavis notes that Keats had

an energy lacking in Dante Gabriel Rossetti (R, 210). With his characteristic focus on individual words, Leavis indicates that Keats would not
have fondled the word "art" with the preciosity of the Pre-Raphaelites
and poets of the nineties (R, 211). "Victorian romantic poetry is 'literary'
as Keats's is not" (R, 212). Yet, as Leavis honestly observes, "we can ourselves see in Keats (if we can see more too) the great Aesthete—the one
Aesthete of genius" (R, 213). What makes Keats "the one Aesthete of
genius" is that even in a poem as indulgent as "Ode on Melancholy" we
find a counterthrust of vitality, "[t]he sudden burst of freshness is, as it
were, the vitality behind Keats's aestheticism breaking through"
(R, 214).

For Leavis, "[t]he relation between the firmness of art and the firm
grasp on the outer world appears most plainly in the ode *To Autumn.*"
Leavis admires Keats's ability to present the "sensuous richness" of
autumn, without "the least touch of artistic over-ripeness" (R, 215).
Leavis sees the poem as "Shakespearian" and "un-Tennysonian" in its
handling of language, "'moss'd cottage-trees' represents a strength—a
native English strength" (R, 216). The subtlety of Leavis's analysis is
evident in his account of the lines, "'And sometimes like a gleaner thou
dost keep / Steady thy laden head across a brook.' . . . In the step from
the rime-word 'keep,' across (so to speak) the pause enforced by the line-
division, to 'Steady' the balancing movement of the gleaner is enacted"
(R, 216). Leavis stresses the importance of Keats's comment in his letter
to John Hamilton Reynolds of September 22, 1819: "I have given up
Hyperion—there were too many Miltonic inversions in it—Miltonic
verse cannot be written but in an artful, or rather, artist's humour. I
wish to give myself up to other sensations. English ought to be kept up"
(qtd. in R, 218). In Leavis's view, "no rich sap flows" in *Hyperion* (R,
220), but he sees "discipline and self-searching" (R, 221) in Keats's debt
to Dante in the poem's revision. Leavis sees Keats's "personal urgency"
as "completely impersonalized; it has become the life, the informing
spirit, of the profoundest kind of impersonality. There is no element of
self-pity—nothing at all of the obliquely self-regarding" (R, 221). As
Leavis observes, "It was, in the Romantic period, the aesthete who
achieved so un-Byronic and so un-Shelleyan a note in the contemplation
of human suffering—the aesthete no longer an aesthete" (R, 221).

Keats enters, in the revised *Hyperion*, what Leavis calls "the field of
tragic experience" (R, 222).

His own acute and inescapable distresses, including the pain of watching helplessly the suffering of persons dear to him, he can, without feeling them the less, contemplate at the same time from (as it were) the outside, as objects, as facts; and the contemplation of the inevitable and endless human suffering to which his more immediately personal experience leads him has a like impersonal strength. This profound tragic impersonality has its concentrated symbolic expression in the vision of Moneta's face. (R, 222)

Leavis finds "clearly the expression of a rare maturity; the attitude is the product of tragic experience, met by discipline in a very uncommonly strong, sincere, and sensitive spirit" (R, 223). "To Autumn," Leavis notes, was written soon after the abandonment of the revised *Hyperion*. It shows "the relation between Keats's sensuousness and his seriousness, his capacity for rapid development . . . poet and letter-writer are at last one" (R, 223).

Revaluation is the book that confirmed Leavis's reputation as a major critic of English poetry. Together with *New Bearings in English Poetry*, it answers the challenge that Eliot laid down to see the tradition of English poetry in a fresh way. The "dislodgement" of Milton and the revaluation of Donne led to a new way of seeing the past of English poetry in dynamic relation to the present, the new poetry that Eliot was writing. *Revaluation* completed a task that Leavis had been engaged in since committing himself to the serious study of English literature immediately after World War I.

Chapter Four

The Novel as Dramatic Poem: 1933–1970

As early as *How to Teach Reading: A Primer for Ezra Pound* (1933), F. R. Leavis argued that "everything that the novelist does is done with words, here, here and here, and that he is to be judged as an artist (if he is one) for the same kind of reason as the poet is. Poetry works by concentration; for the most part, success or failure is obvious locally, in such passages as can be isolated for inspection" (*HTTR,* 135). This is an early statement of Leavis's idea of "the novel as dramatic poem," which was developed in a series of *Scrutiny* articles in the late 1940s and early 1950s, most of which reappeared in *The Great Tradition: George Eliot, Henry James, and Joseph Conrad* (1948) and *D. H. Lawrence: Novelist* (1955). All but one of the six "novel as dramatic poem" essays were written by Leavis himself.[1] His finest and fullest discussion employing this method of analysis, however, is his essay on *Little Dorrit* that began as the Chichele Lecture at Oxford in 1964 and was published in *Dickens the Novelist* (1970). It is this essay that I would like to consider in detail in this chapter.[2] However, it is necessary first to discuss the development of the idea itself from its inception circa 1933.

Leavis's idea of the novel as dramatic poem is related to his belief, expressed in 1952 in an article in *Commentary,* "The Americanness of American Literature," that "[i]n the nineteenth century the strength—the poetic strength—of the English language went into prose fiction. . . . if depth, range, and subtlety in presentment of human experience are the criteria, prose fiction in English between Jane Austen and D. H. Lawrence has a creative achievement to show that is unsurpassed—unsurpassed by any of the famous great phases or chapters of literary history."[3] A thread of continuity between *Revaluation* (1936) and Leavis's criticism of the novel can be seen in *Scrutiny,* in which the essays that formed his chapters on Joseph Conrad and George Eliot in *The Great Tradition* appeared first as "Revaluations" 14 (1941) and 15 (1945–1946).

In an essay called "The Teaching of Literature (3): The Literary Discipline and Liberal Education" (1947), Leavis expressed the view that "the analysis of short things can be developed . . . into more extended and comprehensive criticism."[4] The first essay—on *Hard Times*—of The Novel as Dramatic Poem series, appeared in *Scrutiny* in 1947. So, the idea took shape between 1933 and 1947 when it became explicit. As M. B. Kinch, William Baker, and John Kimber note, in summarizing P. J. M. Robertson's *The Leavises on Fiction* (1981), "[t]he concept signified that the greatest novels are best understood not as linear prose narratives of character and plot, but as dramatic prose-poems having the kind of metaphoric power and complexity of organization found in a Shakespeare play."[5] R. P. Bilan calls Leavis's work on the novel "his most distinctive and original contribution to modern literary criticism," and his essay on *Little Dorrit* the "most ambitious and impressive piece of criticism Leavis has ever written."[6]

As indicated, Leavis wrestled with the question of appropriate methods of criticism for fiction as early as 1933. In his Introduction to *Towards Standards of Criticism,* a compilation of items he chose from *The Calendar of Modern Letters,* he put the question directly: "where is a critic to find help with 'principles' in criticizing fiction . . . ? With little more than a few hints from Henry James—from the prefaces and *Notes on Novelists*—he will have to do everything for himself" (*TSOC,* 15–16). Or would have to, Leavis points out, were it not for the excellent criticism of fiction in *The Calendar of Modern Letters* and C. H. Rickword's "A Note on Fiction" in which, in similar vein to Leavis in *How to Teach Reading*, Rickword remarks that "the problem of language, the use of the medium in all its aspects, is the basic problem of any work of literature" (*TSOC,* 16).

Discussing Rickword's ideas about the criticism of the novel, Leavis gets to the heart of what he believes criticism to be. "Criticism . . . must be in the first place (and never cease being) a matter of sensibility, of responding sensitively and with precise discrimination to the words on the page" (*TSOC,* 17). He quotes Rickword at length, and the quotation appears to contain the origin of the idea of the novel as dramatic poem in Rickword's connection of the novel to drama:

> the form of a novel only exists as a balance of response on the part of the reader. Hence schematic plot is a construction of the reader's that corresponds to an aspect of that response and stands in merely diagrammatic relation to the source. Only as precipitate from the memory are plot or character tangible; yet only in solution have either any emotive valency. The composition of this fluid is a technical matter. The technique of the

novel is just as symphonic as the technique of the drama and as dependent, up to a point, on the dynamic devices of articulation and control of
narrative tempo. But though dependent, it is dependent as legs are on
muscles, for the *how* but not the *why* of movement; and, interesting as
functional technique may be to the mechanical minded and to workers in
the same medium on the look-out for tips, the organic is the province of
criticism. (qtd. in *TSOC,* 17)

Rickword sees similarity between the novel and the drama, and so does
Leavis. "The problem is," as Leavis notes, "to go beyond the words on
the page without losing touch with them; to develop a technique for
keeping the sensibility always in control in one's inevitable dealings
with abstractions and 'precipitates from the memory' " (*TSOC,* 18).

As well as connecting drama and the novel, Leavis believes that the
"bringing together of fiction and poetry is the more richly suggestive
because of the further assimilation it instigates. The differences between
a lyric, a Shakespeare play, and a novel, for some purposes essential, are
in no danger of being forgotten; what needs insisting on is the community. And this for the sake not merely of critical principle, but of immediate profit in critical technique (principle that does not bear on technique is of little interest)" (*TSOC,* 19–20). In this connection, Leavis
also believes that "if one is not intelligent about poetry one is unlikely to
be intelligent about fiction, and the connoisseur of fiction who disclaims
an interest in poetry is probably not interested in literature" (*TSOC,* 21).

At least from *Fiction and the Reading Public* (1932) on, Leavis maintained that Q. D. Leavis was the family expert on the novel. Indeed, *The
Great Tradition* might well have been a joint endeavor as *Dickens the Novelist* was later to be. However, whether the idea of the novel as dramatic
poem was worked out with Q. D. Leavis or not, it emerged slowly. We
have seen that Leavis believed in approaching the novel in this way as
early as 1933 yet did not initiate The Novel as Dramatic Poem series in
Scrutiny until 1947, a year before *The Great Tradition* appeared. The first
essay in the series became the final chapter in *The Great Tradition,* as
"*Hard Times:* An Analytic Note."

Leavis begins his study of *Hard Times* by questioning the traditional
approach to the novel in terms of the novelist creating "a world," "living" characters and lots of "life."[8] He immediately notes the neglect,
along with that of *Hard Times,* of Henry James's *The Europeans,* both
novels that he regards as moral fables. (*The Europeans* was to be the subject of Leavis's second study in The Novel as Dramatic Poem series.)

Leavis defines "the moral fable" by noting that "in it the intention is peculiarly insistent, so that the representative significance of everything in the fable—character, episode, and so on—is immediately apparent as we read" (*GT,* 250). He observes that in Dickens's novels "intention is often very insistent . . . without its being taken up in any inclusive significance that informs and organizes a coherent whole" (*GT,* 250). What distinguishes *Hard Times* as a "dramatic poem" is its poetic concentration, "the Dickensian vitality is there, in its varied characteristic modes, which have the more force because they are free of redundance: the creative exuberance is controlled by a profound inspiration" (*GT,* 250). In *Hard Times,* Leavis finds Dickens "for once possessed by a comprehensive vision, one in which the inhumanities of Victorian civilization are seen as fostered and sanctioned by a hard philosophy, the aggressive formulation of an inhumane spirit" (*GT,* 250). So, the elements of "moral fable," "profound inspiration" and "comprehensive vision" are immediately established as key elements of the novel as dramatic poem.

In *Hard Times,* Dickens's "comprehensive vision" reveals how Thomas Gradgrind's Utilitarianism in association with Josiah Bounderby's "'rugged individualism' in its grossest and most intransigent form'" (*GT,* 250) lead to human disaster. As part of this depiction, Dickens shows the adverse effect of "the Utilitarian spirit in Victorian education" (*GT,* 251) in his presentation of Sissy Jupe's inability to "define" a horse. As Leavis notes, "Bitzer, the model pupil, on the button's being pressed, promptly vomits up the genuine article" (*GT,* 252). On the other hand, Leavis writes of Sissy's "sovereign and indefeasible humanity: it is the virtue that makes it impossible for her to understand or acquiesce in, an ethos for which she is 'girl number twenty,' or to think of any other human being as a unit for arithmetic" (*GT,* 252). Necessary to the moral fable and to the novel as dramatic poem, Leavis finds that Dickens's "ironic method" "associates quite congruously, such is the flexibility of Dickens's art, with very different methods; it cooperates in a truly dramatic and profoundly poetic whole" (*GT,* 253). Far from being "a merely conventional *persona*" Sissy Jupe is "established in a potently symbolic role: she is part of the poetically-creative operation of Dickens's genius in *Hard Times*" (*GT,* 253). Dickens's contrast between Sissy and Bitzer is, for Leavis, "representative of Dickens's art in general in *Hard Times* —with which the moral and spiritual differences are rendered . . . in terms of sensation, so that the symbolic intention emerges out of metaphor and the vivid evocation of the concrete" (*GT,* 253). This focus upon the dramatization of "moral and spiritual differences"

through "metaphor and the vivid evocation of the concrete" is clearly
crucial to the working of the novel as dramatic poem, particularly exemplified in *Hard Times* in Dickens's revealing the different effects of sun-
light on Sissy and Bitzer, caught symbolically at opposite ends of a sun-
beam—Sissy's dark hair and eyes suggesting warmth and life, Bitzer's
light hair and eyes, coldness and death. Gerald Crich's blondness in
Lawrence's *Women in Love* (the subject of Leavis's fourth study in The
Novel as Dramatic Poem series) works in a similar way.

Sissy Jupe's "symbolic significance" is directly linked to Sleary's
"Horse-riding," "where human kindness is very insistently associated with
vitality" (*GT,* 254). Leavis argues that "[t]he way in which the Horse-
riding takes on its significance illustrates beautifully the poetic-dramatic
nature of Dickens's art" (*GT,* 254). His sense of the importance of the relation of the poetic and dramatic in a successful novel is clear enough here.
Leavis brings out the powerful and symbolically resonant contrast that
Dickens draws between the Horse-riding and Stone Lodge and Coketown.
"The Horse-riding, frowned upon as frivolous and wasteful by Gradgrind
and malignantly scorned by Bounderby, brings the machine-hands of
Coketown (the spirit-quenching hideousness of which is hauntingly
evoked) what they are starved of. It brings to them, not merely amuse-
ment, but art, and the spectacle of triumphant activity that, seeming to
contain its end within itself, is, in its easy mastery, joyously self-justified"
(*GT,* 255). Leavis believes that "[i]n investing a travelling circus with this
kind of symbolic value Dickens expresses a profounder reaction to industrialism than might have been expected of him" (*GT,* 255). Also, Leavis
sees Dickens's handling of dialogue in *Hard Times* as often having an
"ironic pointedness" of the kind that we find in "Jonsonian comedy" (*GT,*
257). *Hard Times* is characterized, in Leavis's judgment, by "diversity" and
"irresistible richness of life" that "meets us everywhere, unrestrained and
natural, in the prose" (*GT,* 257). These qualities emerge from Dickens's
"extraordinary energy of perception and registration" (*GT,* 258).

Leavis's sense of *Hard Times* as a successful "dramatic poem" emerges
when he writes of Dickens, "His flexibility is that of a richly poetic art of
the word. He doesn't write 'poetic prose'; he writes with a poetic force of
evocation, registering with the responsiveness of a genius of verbal
expression what he so sharply sees and feels. In fact, by texture, imaginative mode, symbolic method, and the resulting concentration, *Hard
Times* affects us as belonging with formally poetic works" (*GT,* 258).
Although Leavis acknowledges sentimentality in Dickens's characterization of Stephen Blackpool, his general sense is that Dickens "observes

with gusto the humanness of humanity as exhibited in the urban (and suburban) scene. When he sees as he sees so readily, the common manifestations of human kindness, and the essential virtues, asserting themselves in the midst of ugliness, squalor, and banality, his warmly sympathetic response has no disgust to overcome. There is no suggestion, for instance, of recoil—or of distance-keeping—from the game-eyed, brandy-soaked, flabby-surfaced Mr. Sleary, who is successfully made to figure for us a humane anti-Utilitarian positive" (*GT,* 258). Though the handling of Blackpool, Slackbridge and Trade Unionism are unsatisfactory, Sissy Jupe is no Little Nell: "The working of her influence in the Utilitarian home is conveyed with a fine tact, and we do really feel her as a growing potency" (*GT,* 259). Sissy's handling of James Harthouse shows, for Leavis, "The quiet victory of disinterested goodness" that he finds "wholly convincing" (*GT,* 259). Jane Austen's handling of Fanny Price in the Bertram household and Dickens's handling of Sissy Jupe in the Gradgrind household suggest that Dickens read Austen with an intelligent understanding that led to significant influence.

The flexibility of Dickens's art of the novel as dramatic poem in *Hard Times* is further revealed, for Leavis, in the contrast between the "Jonsonian character" of Bounderby, who remains unchanged, and Gradgrind, who "has to *experience* the confutation of his philosophy, and to be capable of the change involved in admitting that life has proved him wrong" (*GT,* 260). In the scene in which Gradgrind presents Bounderby's marriage proposal to Louisa, Dickens achieves what Leavis considers "a triumph of ironic art" (*GT,* 262), whereas in Tom's exposure, Leavis notes "sardonic comedy, imagined with great intensity and done with the sure touch of genius" (*GT,* 265). Indeed, he sees "in the whole effect, a sardonic-tragic in which satire consorts with pathos. *Hard Times* is a poetic work. It suggests that the genius of the writer may fairly be described as that of a poetic dramatist, and that, in our preconceptions about 'the novel,' we may miss, within the field of fictional prose, possibilities of concentration and flexibility in the interpretation of life such as we associate with Shakespearean drama" (*GT,* 266). Here we come as close as possible to a definition of the novel as dramatic poem. "Poetic" and "flexibility" are two of the crucial terms in this description. Leavis also provides readers with substantial quotations from the novel to allow them to appreciate for themselves the working of Dickens's metaphoric, symbolic, ironic, and, above all, poetic art.

The culmination of Dickens's art in *Hard Times* belongs, Leavis writes, "to Dickensian high-fantastic comedy. And there follows the

solemn moral of the whole fable, put with the rightness of genius into
Mr. Sleary's asthmatic mouth" (*GT,* 268). Leavis quotes Sleary: " 'It
seemth to prethent two thingth to a perthon, don't it, Thquire?' said
Mr. Sleary, musing as he looked down into the depths of his brandy-and-
water: 'one, that there ith a love in the world, not all Thelf-intereth after
all, but thomething very different; t'other, that it hath a way of ith own
of calculating or not calculating, which thomehow or another ith at
leatht ath hard to give a name to, ath the wayth of the dogth ith!' " (*GT,*
269). Leavis notes that Shakespeare and Dickens were both popular
entertainers, and that Dickens, like Shakespeare, could create, as in the
ending of *Hard Times,* a "subtle interplay of diverse elements, a multi-
plicity in unison of timbre and tone . . . passages of this characteristic
quality in their relation, a closely organized one, to the poetic whole"
(*GT,* 270).

Despite his high estimate of *Hard Times,* Leavis is not uncritical of it.
Besides, the inadequacy of Dickens's handling of Blackpool, Slackbridge, and Trade Unionism, he is not impressed by Dickens's inability
to realize the important role that religion would have played in the life
of Coketown or by his dismissal of Parliament as the "national dust-
yard" (*GT,* 271), though he does think that "Dickens's understanding of
Victorian civilization is adequate for his purpose" (*GT,* 271).

In concluding his discussion, Leavis praises Dickens's "dramatic creation and imaginative genius" (*GT,* 274). *Hard Times* possesses, for him,
"packed richness . . . almost incredibly varied" (*GT,* 272). For Leavis,
Dickens is a creative writer of Shakespearean quality:

> The final stress may fall on Dickens's command of word, phrase, rhythm,
> and image: in ease and range there is surely no greater master of English
> except Shakespeare. This comes back to saying that Dickens is a great
> poet: his endless resource in felicitously varied expression is an extraordi-
> nary responsiveness to life. His senses are charged with emotional energy,
> and his intelligence plays and flashes in the quickest and sharpest percep-
> tion. That is, his mastery of "style" is of the only kind that matters—
> which is not to say that he hasn't a conscious interest in what can be done
> with words; many of his felicities could plainly not have come if there
> had not been in the background, a habit of such interest." (*GT,* 272)

Leavis's study of *Hard Times* as a dramatic poem was the first in a series
of studies of major novels in similar terms: of James's *The Europeans,* of
Lawrence's *The Rainbow, Women in Love,* and *St. Mawr.* His study of *Hard
Times* initiated, also, his revaluation of Dickens; his subsequent studies of

Dombey and Son and *Little Dorrit* were further studies of Dickens's novels as dramatic poems.

Before discussing "Blake and Dickens: *Little Dorrit*," however, it will be useful to consider Leavis's essay on *The Europeans* to see if it is possible to note any further dimensions to his idea of the novel as dramatic poem than can be discovered from looking closely at his "Analytic Note" on *Hard Times*.

Like *Hard Times,* Henry James's *The Europeans* is, for Leavis, "wholly and intensely significant."[8] The way in which he describes *The Europeans* as a "moral fable" could be applied with equal relevance to *Hard Times*: "a serious intention expresses itself in so firm and clear an economy of organization, and the representative significance of every element in the book is so insistent" (*"E,"* 58). Leavis views *The Europeans* as "a comparative inquiry, enacted in dramatic and poetic terms, into the criteria of civilization" (*"E,"* 58). As with *Hard Times,* "critical irony" emerges as a crucial element. Though in a subtler way than *Hard Times, The Europeans* is structured upon contrasting ways of life. In *Hard Times* we found Utilitarianism (Gradgrindism) opposed to the Horse-riding, while in *The Europeans* Felix's vitality helps to liberate Gertrude from New England Puritanism. However, when we consider the limitation of Eugenia, we realize that there is no simple contrast in James's novel. Pointed dialogue is also important in *The Europeans,* as it was in *Hard Times;* Leavis quotes Felix and Mr. Wentworth's conversation and misunderstanding over Clifford's suspension from Harvard and Felix's misunderstood suggestion that Clifford "make love" to Eugenia.

Both Europe and New England are submitted to James's "critical irony." The contrast between the two is nowhere more subtly and movingly brought out than in Eugenia's response to the Wentworths' home. As Leavis notes:

> In the strength of the first impression, before she has had time to be bored, she pays, embodiment of worldliness that she is, an even more significant tribute:
>
>> There were tears in her eyes. The luminous interior, the gentle tranquil people, the simple, serious life—the sense of these things pressed upon her with an overmastering force, and she felt herself yielding to one of the most genuine emotions she had ever known. "I should like to stay here," she said. "Pray take me in." (*"E,"* 65)

Eugenia, of course, hopes to improve upon her "morganatic" European marriage with an offer from New Englander Robert Acton. How-

ever, while she allows Clifford Wentworth to "court" her to improve his
manners, Clifford ends up proposing to Robert's sister Lizzie, while
Robert rejects Eugenia because he is unable to trust her. The limitations
and strengths of Europe and New England emerge through James's
subtly realized human drama. However, such bald summary fails to provide a just account of the success of James's art in *The Europeans*. As
Leavis remarks, "When we elicit judgments and valuations from the
fable—which is perfectly dramatic and perfectly a work of art—we
don't think of them as coming from the author. It is a drawback of the
present kind of commentary that it tends in some ways to slight this
quality of art, this creative perfection; it doesn't suggest the concrete
richness and self-sufficiency of the drama, or the poetic subtlety of the
means by which the discriminations are established" (*"E,"* 70). Of *The
Europeans,* he notes "the sensitive precision, the closeness of organization
combined with flexibility, of the art everywhere" (*"E,"* 72). As Leavis
observes further, "[t]he 'democracy' that James endorses gets its definition in the whole dramatic poem" (*"E,"* 72). James supports "The Wentworth virtues of sincerity and moral refinement—virtues ideally, his art
implies, separable from the restrictive aspects of Puritanism" (*"E,"* 72).
However, the "Puritan heritage" contains a "steady underlying seriousness" by which the Baroness's duplicity is judged. As Leavis notes, "This
seriousness, it is implied, has its essential part in the ethos of the ideal
civilization" (*"E,"* 72).

As with *Hard Times,* metaphor and symbolism play an important part
in *The Europeans* as "a dramatic poem." Leavis points out that "[t]he
respects in which, for all its indispensable virtues, James finds New
England lacking are suggested by the symbolic parlour into which Felix,
calling for the first time, is led by Gertrude: it is 'a high, clean, rather
empty-looking room.' Imagery of this poetic kind, arising with inevitable
naturalness in the presentment of the drama, plays a great part in the
definition of theme and attitude" (*"E,"* 72). In contrast, the Baroness dec-
orates "the little white house" in which Mr. Wentworth accommodates
her with shawls and draperies. As Leavis notes "the symbolism needs no
explaining" (*"E,"* 73). However, "[i]t is not the Baroness, but her brother
Felix, who represents the important things for lack of which James's New
England has to figure as 'rather empty-looking' " (*"E,"* 73). Felix "stands
for an attitude towards life and for the un-Puritanic 'Bohemian' virtues.
But he stands too for a conception of art and of its function in a civilized
community—that function of which the Wentworths (Gertrude had
never seen a play) are so sadly unaware" (*"E,"* 73).

Concluding his discussion of *The Europeans,* Leavis, with his sense of "the novel as dramatic poem" in view, speaks of "the extraordinarily dramatic quality of the book" (*"E,"* 73). He writes: *"The Europeans* could be very readily adapted for performance. The dialogue—and the action never departs from dialogue—is all admirable 'theatre,' and the whole is done in scenes and situations that seem asking to be acted. The whole, too, in its astonishing economy, is managed with the art of a master dramatist. That culminating twelfth chapter, in which the various constituents of the comedy of personal relations are brought together in a *dénouement,* rivals the admired and comparable things of Shakespeare and Molière" (*"E,"* 73). Finally, Leavis states that *The Europeans* is "[r]ich . . . in symbolic and poetic interest, deep and close" in "its organization as fable and dramatic poem" (*"E,"* 74). Nevertheless, "it can still be read straightforwardly as a novel of manners and social comedy" (*"E,"* 74). Leavis ends by linking James's achievement in *The Europeans* to Jane Austen's: "Jane Austen's novels are known as novels of manners, and, high as her conventional reputation stands, the qualities that make her a great artist have commonly been ignored. Her name comes up naturally and properly here. For in *The Europeans* it is pretty clearly from Jane Austen that James descends; what he offers is a development in the line of *Emma* and *Persuasion*" (*"E,"* 74). It would seem from this that Jane Austen's novels could be profitably reread as "dramatic poems" in Leavis's terms. What are those terms?

From considering Leavis's essays on *Hard Times* and *The Europeans,* it is possible to show that the novel as dramatic poem can be expected to have certain characteristics. Such a novel might well take the form of a moral fable as is the case with Lawrence's *St. Mawr,* though whether *The Rainbow* and *Women in Love* should be read in this way is a more difficult question. A novel that is a dramatic poem should, in Leavis's terms, be a coherent whole, possess poetic concentration that proceeds from "profound inspiration" as well as a "comprehensive form." Though such a novel may employ an ironic method and pointed dialogue, we should expect to discover flexibility in its dramatic presentation. Symbolic method and a poetic art of the word will be evident. Parts will relate to the whole, and the novelist will show ease and range in his command of word, phrase, rhythm, and image.

Though this method of analysis was fully formed by 1948, the year in which *The Great Tradition*—the work that decisively established Leavis as an important critic of the novel—appeared, *Hard Times* was the only work in *The Great Tradition* explicitly treated as a "dramatic poem."

Both George Eliot and Joseph Conrad were subjects of "Revaluations" in *Scrutiny* between 1941 and 1946. In the case of George Eliot, Leavis carefully discriminated between what he saw as the strong and weak elements in her work. He praised the dramatic and sometimes tragic novelist who with disinterested and sensitive awareness gave us Mrs. Poyser's kitchen in *Adam Bede* (1859), the world of St. Ogg's in *The Mill on The Floss* (1860), the tragic Transome theme in *Felix Holt* (1866), the Bulstrode and Lydgate theme in *Middlemarch* (1871–1872), and the Gwendolyn Harleth tragedy in *Daniel Deronda* (1874–1876). He also criticized the idealization of Adam Bede, Felix Holt, and Will Ladislaw and the self-idealization or self-indulgent identification of George Eliot with Maggie Tulliver and Dorothea Brooke. In the case of Conrad he identified a series of major novels running from *Nostromo* (1904) through *The Secret Agent* (1907), *Under Western Eyes* (1911), *Chance* (1913), and *Victory* (1915). With Henry James, Leavis argued for the importance of *Portrait of a Lady* (1881) and some of the early and middle novels over the later work. Altogether, he delineated a "great tradition" of the English novel that, beginning with Jane Austen, developed through the major novels of George Eliot, Henry James and Joseph Conrad. With the establishment of the idea of the novel as dramatic poem, however, Leavis initiated awareness of a line of great creative writers that began with Shakespeare, led to Blake, and continued in the novels of Dickens and Lawrence.

Leavis's "Dickens and Blake: *Little Dorrit*" is one of his finest pieces of literary criticism. It is, also, a study of the novel as dramatic poem. More like the essays on *The Rainbow* and *Women in Love* than the essays on *Hard Times, The Europeans,* and *St. Mawr,* it provides as full as possible a critical account of Dickens's novel. Leavis begins:

> Yet that [*Little Dorrit*] is one of the very greatest of novels—that its omission from any brief list of the great European novels would be critically indefensible—is not a commonplace. The significance focused with a sharp economy in *Hard Times*—a significance the force and bearing of which can't be too insistently impressed on an age of statistical method, social studies and the computer—is at the deep centre of *Little Dorrit;* but published commentary on Dickens doesn't encourage the recognition that any book of his *has* a deep centre. *Little Dorrit* is one that has; it exhibits a unifying and controlling life such as only the greatest kind of creative writer can command. (DN, 213)

Though he does not "offer to elaborate the parallel," Leavis sees a strong one between "Shakespeare's development and achievement as the great popular playwright of our dramatic efflorescence and Dickens's as the marvellously fertile, supremely successful and profoundly creative exploiter of the Victorian market for fiction" (*DN,* 214).

Leavis argues that "just as Shakespeare could be both the established favourite of the groundlings in the popular theatre and the supreme poetic mind of the Renaissance, master explorer of human experience, so Dickens, pursuing indefatigably his career as best-selling producer of popular fiction, could develop into a creative writer of the first order, the superlatively original creator of his art" (*DN,* 214). He sees *Little Dorrit* as a consummate achievement, Dickens's most successful novel to that point: "the whole working of the plot, down to the melodramatic dénouement, is significant" (*DN,* 215). Like Blake, Dickens, in Leavis's view, is a defender of art: "What Dickens hated in the Calvinistic commercialism of the early and middle Victorian age—the repressiveness towards children, the hard righteousness, the fear of love, the armed rigour in the face of life—he sums up now in its hatred of art" (*DN,* 215).

That *Little Dorrit* is unquestionably for Leavis a dramatic poem is made clear when, considering Little Dorrit herself, he writes: "Her genius is to be always beyond question genuine—real. She is indefeasibly real, and the test of reality for others. That is a proposition to which the dramatic poem gives the clearest meaning" (*DN,* 226). At the center of a complex major novel, she has a reality and believability that Little Nell (for Leavis a sentimental cipher) never attains. Near the close of his discussion, Leavis states: "It is impossible to discuss Amy Dorrit as disinterestedness (and the creative nisus that placed her at the centre of *Little Dorrit* is intrinsically normative) without being brought to an explicit recognition that the disinterested individual life, the creative identity, is of its nature a responsibility towards what can't be possessed" (*DN,* 269). Though not an artist, Little Dorrit is creative in her very being. As Leavis puts it, "Little Dorrit, whom I have called a contrasting opposite to Gowan the nihilist, is not only *not* an artist, she hasn't the makings of an artist in her. It is in her *being*—being what she is—that she is creative" (*DN,* 236).

In reading *Little Dorrit,* Leavis notes seven key words: "reality, courage, disinterestedness, truth, spontaneity, creativeness—life" (*DN,* 237). These, for Leavis, are the crucial positives that *Little Dorrit* enacts. He keeps his readers aware of the significance of these words throughout his study of the novel. Early on he quotes D. H. Lawrence from "Morality and the Novel": "The novel is the highest example of subtle interrelatedness that man has discovered" (qtd. in *DN,* 227). In many ways

"Dickens and Blake: *Little Dorrit*" can be described as a study of "subtle inter-relatedness" in Dickens's novel. Leavis speaks of the difficulty of attempting to group the characters in the novel for critical consideration, "so that, if in our diagrammatic notation we have been representing groupings by lines linking names, the lines run across one another in an untidy and undiagrammatic mess. The diagrammatic suggestion is soon transcended as the growing complexity of lines thickens; we arrive at telling ourselves explicitly what we have been implicitly realizing in immediate perception and response: 'This, brought before us for pondering contemplation, is life—life as it manifests itself variously in this, that and the other focusing individual (the only way in which it can)'" (*DN*, 217–18).

Nevertheless, Leavis's method in the essay is to consider each of the novel's central characters and the "subtle inter-relatedness" of characters to each other. I have already discussed the centrality that Leavis accords to the novel's titular heroine. In fact, Leavis discusses Arthur Clennam before he discusses Little Dorrit. He likens Dickens's handling of Clennam to his handling of Pip in *Great Expectations;* as with Pip so through Clennam we see the events of the novel. Both characters are in some respects foci for the reader (*DN*, 218). However, both change through the course of their respective novels; through the agency of Little Dorrit, Clennam overcomes his lack of will; he is regenerated through her love. Leavis argues that Clennam acts as "the reader's immediate presence in the book" (*DN*, 237).

In contrast to Little Dorrit, whose creative being is suffused through the novel, Leavis sees Mrs. Clennam as representing the clenched, sabbatarian Calvinistic will. He shows well how the novel is built upon a series of "subtly-interrelated," yet contrasting, characters. Henry Gowan is the unreal artist whose laziness, arrogance, and cynicism flout art, whereas Daniel Doyce is an inventor whose attitude to good work is selfless. Doyce seems like a model for Caleb Garth in *Middlemarch*. He is like the character Physician of whom Leavis notes that it is remarked, "where he was, something real was" (*DN*, 240). Leavis also considers the vitality in Flora Finching's free-flowing speech, as well as Pancks's wonderful exposure of Casby. All these characters are woven by Dickens into a novel that, for Leavis, reaches "beyond moral-fable economy" (*DN*, 247) of the kind he analyzed in *Hard Times* and *The Europeans* to form what he calls its "total significance," the "essential communication of the book" (*DN*, 263).

Leavis notes James's debt to *Little Dorrit* in *The Princess Casamassima* (1886). He sees Dickens as clearly a greater artist than James (*DN*, 248). For Leavis, Dickens reveals a Shakespearean abundance, flexibility, and power. In *Little Dorrit*, Leavis sees the William Dorrit and Merdle characters and involvements as close to tragic. The relation between William Dorrit and his daughter Amy has something of the Lear-Cordelia relationship to it. Dickens's prose is, for Leavis, the finest expressive vehicle since Shakespeare's blank verse (*DN*, 265). In fact, Dickens is a poet whose major novels—*Dombey and Son, David Copperfield, Bleak House, Hard Times, Little Dorrit, Great Expectations,* and *Our Mutual Friend*—are best read as dramatic poems. For Leavis, Dickens is a "greater poet than any of the Victorian formal poets" (*DN*, 253). Dickens's depiction of Rome in *Little Dorrit* becomes the inspiration for George Eliot's similar depiction in *Middlemarch*, as well as for Henry James's in *Portrait of a Lady*.

Dickens's dramatic inquiry into Victorian snobbery and the nature of gentlemanliness is, for Leavis, brilliantly achieved through such characters as Ferdinand Barnacle and Blandois. He sees Dickens, in conclusion, as the great romantic novelist (*DN*, 276), and Romanticism, for Leavis, was a far greater positive achievement than T. S. Eliot believed it to be. As the great Romantic novelist, Dickens, in his relationship with his audience, understood "the collaborative nature of creativity" (*DN*, 273) better than Blake. But throughout the essay, one of Leavis's most persuasive and powerful pieces of critical writing, he draws a striking connection between Blake and Dickens—Dickens shows the "chartered streets" of England's capital with the same visionary power as Blake does in his poem "London." In Leavis's view, Dickens understands the distinction between "selfhood" and "identity" as clearly as Blake. Both explore Urizenic limitation and celebrate "ego-free love." Blake and Dickens are both strong defenders and celebrants of the essential importance of art in life; both, indeed, vindicate the human spirit that, for Leavis, is life.

Leavis wrote other important essays on the novel following *The Great Tradition* and *D. H. Lawrence: Novelist* on novels such as *Adam Bede, Anna Karenina, Dombey and Son, The Shadow-Line,* and *The Secret Sharer*. He even discusses *The Pilgrim's Progress* as the fountainhead of the English novel.[9] Some of these essays treat the novels as dramatic poems, but, for examples, the *Adam Bede* essay is clearly an introduction to an edition of the novel, whereas the *Anna Karenina* essay is titled "Thought and Significance in a Great Creative Work." He may have felt hesitant about writing of it as a dramatic poem since it was not written in English.

Leavis's approach to the novel as dramatic poem together with his delineation of a great tradition of the English novel are his major contributions to the criticism of the novel. However, beyond the great tradition, Leavis came to perceive a greater vital and visionary tradition that originates with Shakespeare and runs through Blake to Dickens and Lawrence. The last two of these major creative writers are, for Leavis, authors of major novels as dramatic poems.

Chapter Five

Field-Performances: The Higher Pamphleteering and the Third Realm: 1962–1972

Leavis's retirement from full-time lecturing and supervision in 1962 permitted him to take on visiting professorships and give public lectures that he sometimes called "field-performances" (MacKillop, 375). He continued a determined champion of his beliefs expressed in what he called the "higher pamphleteering" (MacKillop, 328). His critical thinking was as sharp as ever and in this period he developed important new ideas such as "the third realm" ("TC," 62). The purpose of this chapter is to explore these developments in Leavis's critical thinking.

Eliot wrote "In my end is my beginning."[1] Leavis with characteristic courage took his retirement as a fresh opportunity. Indeed, the 1960s was one of the most active decades of his career. He was appointed a University Reader in English in 1959, in, as he noted, his 65th year (MacKillop, 299–300). Even before his retirement in 1962 he delivered his most famous public lecture, "Two Cultures? The Significance of C. P. Snow," the Richmond Lecture at Downing College in which he replied with powerful irony to Snow's Rede Lecture "The Two Cultures and the Scientific Revolution," which Cambridge University Press had published in 1959. In 1963 Leavis published a Retrospect to *Scrutiny* when Cambridge University Press republished the journal that Leavis had edited from 1932 until 1953. The Retrospect provided a summing up of one part of his career. The following year he gave the Chichele Lecture at All Souls College, Oxford, on *Little Dorrit,* which became a chapter of *Dickens the Novelist* (1970). He resigned his Downing College fellowship the same year. In 1965 Leavis accepted a visiting professorship at the then new University of York. *"Anna Karenina" and other Essays,* which he published in 1967, was dedicated to that university. In it he gathered many essays, particularly on the novel, that he had written since the publication of *The Great Tradition.* During 1965, F. R. and Q. D. Leavis gave British Council sponsored lectures and seminars in Finland. The following year they lectured at Cornell and Harvard universities. These lectures were published in 1969 as *Lectures in America*. In 1967 Leavis was invited to deliver the Clark Lectures at Trinity College, Cambridge. They appeared, also in 1969, as *English Literature in Our Time and the University*. During 1969 Leavis was a visiting professor at the University of Wales and University of Bristol. Lectures given there and at the University of York, as well as previous lectures given at Downing and in the United States, completed a decade of advocacy and fresh discovery when they appeared as *Nor Shall My Sword: Discourses on Pluralism, Compassion, and Social Hope* in 1972, when Leavis was 77.

My purpose in the present chapter is to discuss the "Two Cultures" lecture and its development into the lectures gathered in *Nor Shall My Sword*. My aim is to show how Leavis's "field-performances" and works of "higher pamphleteering" moved together with new developments in his critical thinking. "Two Cultures" was published in *The Spectator* in 1962 and stirred nationwide controversy. It appeared in book form in the same year and then opened *Nor Shall My Sword* a decade later.

"Two Cultures? The Significance of Lord Snow" begins with Leavis's best known sentence: "If confidence in oneself as a master-mind, qualified by capacity, insight and knowledge to pronounce authoritatively on the frightening problems of our civilization, is genius, then there can be no doubt about Sir Charles Snow's" ("TC," 41). The Richmond Lecture, given on February 28, 1962, bristles with irony. Leavis states Snow's "position" briefly: "The general nature of his position and his claim to authority are well known: there are the two un-communicating and mutually indifferent cultures, there is the need to bring them together, and there is C. P. Snow, whose place in history is that he has them both, so that we have in him, the paradigm of the desired and necessary union" ("TC," 44). In addition to his observations on the marked differences in the body of knowledge of the "literary intellectual" and the scientist, Snow makes broad generalizations about the difference in social and political attitude between the members of his "two cultures." Without using supporting evidence, Snow argues that scientists tend to be politically left wing, with positive, progressive social attitudes and a concern for the poor of the world. He associates literary intellectuals with reactionary politics, social stasis, and attitudes of withdrawal from the problems of society or a lack of compassion toward the poor of the world. While arguing for a rapprochement between his "two cultures," Snow is hostile to what he terms the "literary culture." He argues that "Western intellectuals have never tried, wanted or been able to under-

stand the industrial revolution, much less accept it. Intellectuals, in particular literary intellectuals, are natural Luddites."[2] His attack on mod-
ernism is even more marked. Snow quotes an unnamed "scientist of distinction" to the effect that "nine out of ten of those who have dominated
literary sensibility in our time—weren't they not only politically silly,
but politically wicked? Didn't the influence of all they represent bring
Auschwitz that much nearer?" (Snow, 7). Snow argues (while making
Yeats an exception to the charge) that "the correct answer was not to
defend the indefensible. . . . It was no use denying the facts, which are
broadly true" (Snow, 8). He does argue, however, that "it is ill-considered
of scientists to judge writers on the evidence of the period 1914–50"
(Snow, 8). On the other hand, he argues that scientists "are freer than
most people from racial feeling; their own culture is in its human relations a democratic one" (Snow, 48).

Leavis deplores Snow's argument that there is a literary culture and a
scientific culture, as he deplores Snow's distinction between the tragic
condition of the individual and the "social hope" he offers to society in
the form of improved material standards of living powered by technological advances. In Leavis's view, Snow's discussion reveals an ignorance
of the nature of culture, and of the centrality of language (and literature)
in the formation of culture. For Leavis "there is a prior human achievement of collaborative creation, a more basic work of the mind of man
(and more than the mind), one without which the triumphant erection
of the scientific edifice would not have been possible: that is, the creation of the human world, including language" ("TC," 61).

Leavis's deepest scorn is reserved for the "crass Wellsianism" of
Snow's account of the history of the industrial revolution. His blunt
response to his quotation from Snow is characteristic of Leavis's Richmond Lecture: " 'For, with singular unanimity, in any country where
they have had the chance, the poor have walked off the land into the
factories as fast as the factories could take them.' This, of course, is mere
brute assertion, callous in its irresponsibility" ("TC," 57). Leavis argues
that "the actual history has been, with significance for one's apprehen-
sion of the full human problem, incomparably and poignantly more
complex" ("TC," 57) than Snow claims.

Leavis is opposed to Snow's materialism and the crudely patronizing
language in which it is expressed. Snow's emphasis on "productivity,
material standards of living, hygienic and technological progress"
("TC," 52) disregards concerns that Leavis believes are a necessary part
of our humanity and that are critically important for our future. How-

ever, those who question the human cost involved in the material advancement offered by science are characterized by Snow as "natural Luddites" ("TC," 57). In Leavis's view, Snow includes the great creative writers of the nineteenth and twentieth centuries, such as Dickens and Ruskin, in this caricature. Yet as Leavis points out, "it was Ruskin who put into currency the distinction between wealth and well-being, which runs down through Morris and the British socialist movement to the Welfare State" ("TC," 57–58). Snow, Leavis argues, has failed to grasp this distinction as he has failed to understand the importance of the spiritual values for which Ruskin and Dickens stand.

Leavis asserts that Snow, in arguing for the existence of two cultures—literary and scientific—misuses the word culture. By "literary culture," Leavis argues, Snow means the world of the "literary intellectual," the *New Statesman,* and the Sunday papers. Snow, Leavis suggests, regards this "culture" as "representing the age's finer consciousness so far as a culture ignorant of science can" ("TC," 48). Leavis finds Snow's idea of what constitutes "literary culture" inimical. He attacks Snow's judgment of individual artists when he notes the omission of D. H. Lawrence from Snow's catalogue of "the writers who above all matter" and the inclusion of "the brutal and boring Wyndham Lewis" ("TC," 53). Snow, in Leavis's view, exhibits a "blankness in the face of literature" ("TC," 55). He fails to understand that "literature has its immediate and crucial relevance" because of writers who ask in their work, "What ultimately do men live by? These questions are in and of the creative drive that produces great art in Conrad and Lawrence (to instance two very different novelists of the century who haven't, one gathers, impressed Snow)" ("TC," 55–56).

While Leavis attacks Snow personally, he is also attacking the literary, intellectual establishment of which he sees Snow as representative. Leavis regards Snow as, "in himself negligible." However, the fact that his ideas have been positively received, praised, and respected is, for Leavis, a sign of the intellectual poverty of that establishment. It was the realization, upon marking examination papers, that Snow's ideas were being disseminated in schools, and that students were being encouraged to read Snow "as doctrinal, definitive and formative" ("TC," 43–44) that prompted Leavis to respond to Snow's lecture. For Leavis, Snow's lecture, far from being worthy to be recommended to school students as "a trenchant formulation to a key contemporary truth" ("TC," 43) could be used "as a text for elementary criticism; criticism of the style, here, becomes, as it follows down into analysis, criticism of the thought, the essence, the pretensions" ("TC," 44). Leavis notes the frequent use by Snow of clichés such as "history is merciless to failure" and "they have the future in their bones" ("TC," 51), and the careless way in which Snow "without any sense of there having been a shift, slips from his 'literary culture' into 'the traditional culture'" ("TC," 49). Leavis is particularly incensed by "the callously ugly insensitiveness" of Snow's language when he addresses the desire for material prosperity in human life. He quotes Snow directly: "Jam today, and men aren't at their most exciting: jam tomorrow, and one often sees them at their noblest" (qtd. in "TC," 58). Snow, Leavis argues, ignores Ruskin's distinction between wealth and well-being and equates "salvation and lasting felicity" with the acquisition of "jam" ("TC," 59).

Anticipating charges that he is a "natural Luddite," Leavis insists that he is not advocating any attempt to defy or turn the clock back on technological advance or scientific education. His argument is that an exclusive attention to the material is "disastrously not enough" ("TC," 59). Members of societies who enjoy material prosperity and advanced technology are not "more fully human" than people who live without those benefits. Advancing technology, he argues, will bring "tests and challenges so unprecedented" that humankind will need not "traditional wisdom" but all its resources of "creative response" to face them ("TC," 60–61).

In addition to his discussion of the differences between the world views of the "two cultures," and the importance of scientific and technological revolution in materialist terms, Snow argues for changes in the English educational system to produce more scientists and technicians, as well as bureaucrats with enough education in science to allow them to make more intelligent policy decisions in a society changed by the scientific revolution and the technologies produced by it. In all this, Snow appears to see a diminishing public role for the "literary culture." Countering Snow's assertion that "the scientific edifice of the physical world" is "in its intellectual depth, complexity and articulation, the most beautiful and wonderful collective work of the mind of man" ("TC," 61), Leavis argues that "the creation of the human world, including language" is a "prior human achievement of collaborative creation, . . . without which the triumphant erection of the scientific edifice would not have been possible" ("TC," 61).

Leavis refuses to accept Snow's suggested equation between reading a Shakespeare play and describing the second law of thermodynamics as exemplary of the "two cultures." Instead he ends by stressing the impor-

tance of the study of literature, for "[i]t is in the study of literature, the
literature of one's own age in the first place, that one comes to recognize
the nature and priority of the third realm (as, unphilosophically, no
doubt, I call it, talking with my pupils), the realm of that which is neither merely private and personal nor public in the sense that it can be
brought into the laboratory and pointed to" ("TC," 62).

The "third realm" described here is central in Leavis's critical thinking. He argues that "[y]ou cannot point to the poem; it is 'there' only in
the re-creative response of individual minds to the black marks on the
page. But—a necessary faith—it is something in which minds can meet.
The process in which this faith is justified is given fairly enough in an
account of the nature of criticism" ("TC," 62). What he comes up with
is that "[a] judgment is personal or it is nothing; you cannot take over
someone else's. The implicit form of a judgment is: This is so, isn't it?
The question is an appeal for confirmation that the thing *is* so; implicitly that, though expecting, characteristically, an answer in the form,
'yes, but—' the 'but' standing for qualifications, reserves, corrections"
("TC," 62).

Leavis sees this formulation of "the nature of criticism" as providing
"a diagram of the collaborative-creative process in which the poem
comes to be established as something 'out there,' of common access in
what is in some sense a public world" ("TC," 62). The same diagram
helps us to understand, too, "the nature of the existence of English literature, a living whole that can have its life only in the living present, in
the creative response of individuals, who collaboratively renew and per-
petuate what they participate in—a cultural community or consciousness. More, it gives us the nature in general of what I have called the
'third realm' to which all that makes us human belongs" ("TC," 62).
This, in essence, is Leavis's answer. Snow's "two cultures" do not exist in
reality. Leavis has described the true nature of "a cultural community or
consciousness" ("TC," 62). "Two Cultures? The Significance of Lord
Snow" provides a paradigm for Leavis's "field-performances" or works of
"higher pamphleteering" of the 1960s as he continued to explore the
issues raised in "Two Cultures?" together with other equally important
matters.

The challenge before us, as Leavis defines it at the close of his Richmond Lecture, is that "for the sake of a human future, we must do, with
intelligent resolution and with faith, all we can to maintain the full life
in the present—and life is growth—of our transmitted culture" ("TC,"
63). Leavis says that, like Snow, he looks to the university to provide

leadership. Unlike Snow, Leavis does not see the university as merely "a collocation of specialist departments" ("TC," 63). Rather, he wishes to see it become "a centre of human consciousness: perception, knowledge, judgment and responsibility" ("TC," 63). For Leavis, "the centre of the university" should be "a vital English School" ("TC," 63); such a school can do crucial "creative work" on "the contemporary intellectual-cultural frontier in maintaining the critical function" ("TC," 64). The university needs to provide "a centre of consciousness (and conscience) for our civilization" ("TC," 64), and be a place "where the culture of the Sunday papers [is] not taken to represent the best that is thought and known in our time" ("TC," 64). If such could become the case, Leavis argues, "the attention I have paid to Snow would be unnecessary" ("TC," 64).

The vehemence of his attack on Snow can be seen as a measure of how important the matters at issue were for Leavis. Certainly the Richmond Lecture brought unprecedented public attention to the dispute between Leavis and Snow. It must be asked, however, if the manner of the attack actually deflected attention from the matter of Leavis's argument.

"Luddites? *or* There is Only One Culture" was delivered at Cornell and Harvard in 1966, four years after the Richmond Lecture. In part, it is a response to the reception of the earlier lecture. Leavis opens by saying, "I am used to being misrepresented, but not resigned to it."[3] The Richmond Lecture had aroused great controversy. Unfortunately, in Leavis's view, he was confronted by "a willed refusal to see and understand" ("Luddites," 77) on the part of some of his audience. It was suggested in the *Partisan Review* that he had not made clear whether he was *for* or *against* a higher standard of living. Leavis, once more, made the point that to concentrate on the achievement of "technological and material advance and fair distribution" ("Luddites," 78) at the expense of all other considerations might well lead us to enjoy our higher standard of living "in a vacuum of disinheritance" ("Luddites," 79).

As before, Leavis objects to great nineteenth-century writers—especially Arnold and Dickens—being dubbed Luddites because of their questioning of technology as a universal solvent. He sees Dickens as standing for "the profoundly relevant creative energy represented by literature" ("Luddites," 81). For Dickens, writing in a period of great change, "sensitive to the full actuality of contemporary life" ("Luddites," 82) was able to represent that life in his work in a way that makes "the histories of the professional social historian seem empty and unenlightening" ("Luddites," 81). *Dombey and Son* reveals how far Dickens was from being a Luddite in its characterization of Toodle, who has benefited from the railway age. Also, Leavis points to the importance of the inventor Daniel Doyce in *Little Dorrit*, "that very great novel which, of all Dickens's larger works, is the most highly organized, everything in it being significant in relation to the whole—and the whole constituting something like an inquest into civilization in contemporary England" ("Luddites," 83).

What Leavis calls "the accelerating technological revolution" ("Luddites," 85) that has destroyed "the organic community" ("Luddites," 55) brings with it "attendant human problem[s]" ("Luddites," 85) that Leavis believes can only be addressed through education, through recreating an educated public capable of sustaining the critical function. Toodles, in *Dombey and Son*, who Dickens "invested with a cheering significance for the human future" ("Luddites," 86) is now faced with automation. The problem for Leavis (and for us) is "[a] general impoverishment of life—that is the threat that, ironically, accompanies the technological advance and the rising standard of living; and we are all involved." ("Luddites," 87).

Leavis reiterates his view that "there is only *one* [English] culture; to talk of *two* in your [Snow's] way is to use an essential term with obviously disqualifying irresponsibility" ("Luddites," 88). Leavis is no happier with Aldous Huxley's "scientism" and "literarism" ("Luddites," 91) than he is with Snow's "two cultures." He fears that by concentrating on such divisions we fail to recognize that humanity "has a need to feel life significant; a hunger for significance that isn't altogether satisfied by devotion to Tottenham Hotspur or by hopes of the World Cup for a team called England or Uruguay, or by space travel (mediated by professional publicists), or by patriotic ardour nourished by international athletics, or by the thrill of broken records" ("Luddites," 92).

What Leavis fears are "the cultural effects of mass-production—in the levelling down that goes with standardization" ("Luddites," 95). To counteract these effects "in an age of revolutionary and constantly advancing technology" ("Luddites," 95) the university must become "a focus of consciousness and human responsibility" ("Luddites," 96). "Luddites? *or* There is Only One Culture" was delivered at Cornell and Harvard, and though Leavis acknowledges that his argument has an English context, he nevertheless believes that Britain and the United States "face in essence one and the same problem" ("Luddites," 96). In both Britain and the United States he wishes to see "'the university as a guarantor of a real performance of the critical function—that critical function which is a creative one'" ("Luddites," 96–97). Though he has been accused of "literarism" ("Luddites," 97), Leavis's reply is that "I don't believe in any 'literary values,' and you won't find me talking about them, the judgments the literary critic is concerned with are judgments about life. What the critical discipline is concerned with is relevance and precision in making and developing them. To think that to have a vital contemporary performance of the critical function matters is to think that creative literature matters; and it matters because to have a living literature, a literary tradition that *lives* in the present—and nothing lives unless it goes on being creative, is to have, as an informing spirit in civilization, an informed, charged and authoritative awareness of inner human nature and human need" ("Luddites," 97).

Leavis concludes by arguing that "the literary-critical judgment is the type of all judgments" ("Luddites," 98). To support the exercise of such judgments, the university as "a real and vital centre of consciousness, should *be* such a public or community as the critic needs, being in that way one of the sustaining creative nuclei of a larger community" ("Luddites," 98).

In the last four articles in *Nor Shall My Sword*—"'English,' Unrest, and Continuity," delivered at Gregynog to an audience from the University of Wales; "'Literarism' versus 'Scientism': the Misconception and the Menace," given at the University of Bristol; "Pluralism, Compassion, and Social Hope" and "Élites, Oligarchies, and an Educated Public," given at the University of York—Leavis continues the arguments raised in the "Two Cultures" controversy. Throughout his career he had urged the need for the creation of an educated public to sustain English culture in the face of the "cultural disinheritance and the meaninglessness of the technologico-Benthamite world."[4] In these articles he focuses on the importance of university education, particularly education in English literature, in the creation of an educated public.

Leavis argues that in spite of existing in a world in which politicians regard "a university as an industrial plant" ("English," 131), universities must struggle to transcend both the clichéd "two categories under which university work falls—contribution to knowledge and communicating knowledge to students" ("English," 108) and "departmental frontiers" ("English," 109), so that it can prepare students to undertake the vital function of criticism in society. This function, in Leavis's view, is to struggle against "'spiritual Philistinism'" and to defend and partake in "that creative human reality of significances, values and nonmensurable ends which our technologico-Benthamite civilization ignores and progressively impoverishes, thus threatening human existence" ("English," 110).

Leavis suggests that for the "English school" to occupy an important place within the university, as he thinks it should, the study of English literature must gain respect as "a discipline of intelligence as genuine as that of any of the sciences and certainly not less important" ("English," 108). He argues, as throughout his career, that literature "has its life in the present or not at all." It is the function of literary criticism to ensure that literature "shall be a living reality" ("English," 112). In performing this function, the student of English should continually confront questions of what constitutes literary history and English literature. Judgments must be made continually and "in genuine personal self-commitment by each student for himself" ("English," 109). An interest in literary history is necessary because, in Leavis's view, contemporary civilization has culturally disinherited the English people and has left them incapacitated as human beings. The study of English literature is important, in part, because it is a discipline that values human creativity and recognizes the contribution the creative artist makes to human society. The need to learn from "the artist's developed creativity" is, Leavis argues, vital for the human future. The true artist's creativity is social as well as individual: "the potently individual such as an artist is discovers, as he explores his most intimate experience, how inescapably social he is in his very individuality. The poet, for instance, didn't create the language without which he couldn't have begun to be a poet, and a language is more than an instrument of expression."[5] In this connection, Leavis believes, it is important to understand the distinction made by William Blake between "identity" and "selfhood": "The individual as 'selfhood' wills egotistically, from his enclosed centre, and is implicitly intent on asserting possession. As creative identity the individual is the agent of life, and 'knows that he does not belong to himself.' He serves something that is quite other than his selfhood, which is blind and blank to it" ("Pluralism," 172). This association of the creative artist with an identity beyond the self, and beyond the material, is crucial to Leavis's conception of cultural continuity and humane society. His fear is that "the drive of our triumphant technologico-Benthamite world is not merely indifferent, but hostile, to human creativity. . . ."[6]

One of the hallmarks of Leavis's criticism is the close attention he pays to language—to the use of individual words. In "Pluralism, Compassion, and Social Hope" he discusses the clichéd use of "the most important words—important for those troubled about the prospect that confronts humanity" ("Pluralism," 163), and the necessity for reclaiming them. His discussion of the use by what he calls the "'humanist' intellectual" (he uses examples from Lord Snow and Lord Annan) of words such as *social, tragic, pluralism,* and *compassion* leads him to a consideration of the use and abuse of the word *élitism.* This word he suggests is "a bad word, a term of condemnation in the progressivist armoury" ("Pluralism," 168). However, Leavis suggests, "nothing is stronger in them [progressivists] than the assumption that *they* are an élite" ("Pluralism," 168). Moreover, he suggests that they are a privileged élite who assume the right to impose policy on those they deem (to use another cliché) "under-privileged" ("Pluralism," 169). Leavis attacks the negative use of the word *élitism* because, he argues, "[t]here are scientist élites, air-pilot élites, *corps d'élite,* and social élites (the best people), and the underprivileged masses know that professional footballers and BBC announcers are élites" ("Pluralism," 169). Furthermore, he argues, "there must always be élites." However, the word "in its progressivist-political use" as a term of condemnation "mobilizing and directing . . . ignorance, prejudice and unintelligence . . . aims at destroying the only adequate control for 'élites' there could be" ("Pluralism," 169).

Leavis spoke with feeling on this subject, perhaps, because his own ideas on education and culture had been attacked as "élitist." He, of course, was concerned that the proposed changes in education in Britain would lead to a serious decline in standards both at the secondary and postsecondary levels. He was also concerned that the increasing reliance on the use of technology in education was another instance of the mechanical taking over from the organic with a resultant loss of human connection. As he puts it in "'Literarism' versus 'Scientism,'" "I am not proposing to ban the computer, but emphasizing the problem of ensuring that the use of the computer shall be really a use—that it shall be used as truly a means in the service of adequately conceived human ends" ("Literarism," 156). Leavis was concerned that the increasing emphasis on technical and scientific education was leading to a devaluation of the arts and of the study of the arts. He regarded it as a "genocidal illusion to suppose that indifference to art and the conditions of it, even though indifference presents itself as zeal for social reform, will improve the lot of humanity."[7]

Finally, in "Élites, Oligarchies, and an Educated Public," Leavis returns to his argument that the only way to sustain culture and to make élites and oligarchies "aware that they are subject to criticism, check and control" ("Elites," 211) is to produce and maintain an educated public. He makes it clear that his idea of an educated public transcends preconceived notions of social class, economic position, or political affiliation: "Its importance, in fact, is conditioned by its diversity of presumable bent and its lack of anything like ideological unity." Thus, for Leavis, "the educated class presents its vital unity as essentially a matter of diversities—diversities that make it the public without which there couldn't be the creative differences (rising into creative quarrelling) that maintain the livingness of cultural continuity. It *is* in fact, the presence of the continuity, and *that* constitutes its unity"("Elites," 213). Leavis believed that the university, and the "English school" within it must have a critical role in sustaining an educated public. Further he suggests that a journal, like the reviews of the nineteenth century, or *Scrutiny,* is needed to provide a "real contemporary performance of the critical function" ("Elites," 218). Leavis offers a challenge to his audience to "try whether, in launching a review, it can justify the hope of attracting the contributing connexion needed to keep it going. And, as a matter of fact, there is beyond doubt a good deal of talent that remains undeveloped and unexercised in relation to its most serious interest because there is no organ in which to publish" ("Elites," 218–19). From 1970 to 1974 with *The Human World* and again from 1982 to 1986 with *The Gadfly,* Ian Robinson answered Leavis's challenge. Similarly, Leavis offers a challenge to *The Times* to provide "a regular weekly page of reviewing that included intelligent, coterie-free and boldly disinterested critical attention to current 'literary' publishing" ("Elites," 220).

The final paragraph of "Élites, Oligarchies, and an Educated Public" makes clear where Leavis has stood through *Nor Shall My Sword,* in fact, throughout his career as a literary critic: "let it be explicitly *said,* then, that those who are really, and without illusion, intent on saving the country are consciously, and necessarily, the vindicators and defenders of its greatness, and, as such, are not less essentially opposed to the spirit of those who wish they could believe that Mr. Heath's government will make England great again than they are to the kind of enlightened wisdom personified in Bertrand Russell. The greatness gone, there is nothing left to save, and the loss is humanity's" ("Elites," 227–28).

Nor Shall My Sword has a summative power that shows where Leavis stands and has always stood. However, although it was published when he was 77, Leavis had not finished. Two final encounters, with Eliot (1975) and Lawrence (1976), were to follow before Leavis was willing even to consider laying down the sword.

Chapter Six

"The Long Run In:"
Eliot and Lawrence:
1975–1976

Leavis's critical engagement with the work of T. S. Eliot and D. H. Lawrence was lifelong. He had early been impressed by Eliot's poetry and wrote enthusiastically about it in *New Bearings in English Poetry*. Indeed, Eliot was for Leavis the poet who decisively "altered expression" during and immediately after World War I. In Leavis's view, Eliot did what Wordsworth had done at the beginning of the previous century. However, although Leavis admired a number of Eliot's earlier poems and parts of *Four Quartets*—and thought it Eliot's most important work—as early as 1930 he began to question and distrust Eliot the man, the critic, and the artist. Eliot's criticism of Lawrence deepened Leavis's criticism of Eliot.

Leavis first read Lawrence's short stories in *The English Review* in 1912 when still at school. His admiration for Lawrence grew slowly and lasted his life. In fact, Leavis came to identify closely with Lawrence, who became for him a great novelist and "perfect" critic. Although Leavis had written frequently about Eliot and had written a pamphlet and a book about Lawrence, he felt a need into his eightieth year to clarify his sense of Eliot's and Lawrence's achievements. If the first half of the twentieth-century in English literature was the age of Eliot and Lawrence, it was also the age of Leavis, their principal critic ("Third Realm," 83). In this concluding chapter, I will discuss Leavis's commentary on Eliot's *Four Quartets* in *The Living Principle: "English" As a Discipline of Thought* (1975) and his final discussion of Lawrence in *Thought, Words, and Creativity: Art and Thought in Lawrence* (1976). Before discussing Leavis's account of *Four Quartets* in the third section of *The Living Principle*, however, I will consider the first two sections of the book: "Thought, Language, and Objectivity," and "Judgment and Analysis" (originally published in *Scrutiny* in the mid to late 1940s and early 1950s). In his Preface to the book, Leavis argues that "[i]ntelligent thought about the nature of thought and the criteria of good thinking is impossible apart from intelligence about the nature of language, and the necessary intelligence about language involves an intimate acquaintance with a subtle language in its fullest use. English is a subtle language; its literature is very rich, and its continuity stretches over centuries, starting long before the great seventeenth-century change; so there is point in saying that for the English-speaking philosopher the fullest use of language ought to be its use by the creative writers of his own time, and he needs to take full cognizance of this truth."[1] These are Leavis's reasons "for insisting that the critical discipline—the distinctive discipline of university 'English'—is a discipline of intelligence, and for being explicit and repetitive in associating the word 'intelligence' with the word 'thought'." (*LP,* 13).

Leavis opens the first section of *The Living Principle,* "Thought, Language, and Objectivity" in a disarming way: "this is not the book I have been often reproached with having promised a quarter of a century ago, and never having produced. 'Judgment and Analysis' was the heading I put over some of the intended contents when they were printed in *Scrutiny.* I had coined the phrase as a substitute for 'Practical Criticism' " (*LP,* 19). In this opening section, Leavis goes on to say that what he means by practical criticism is "criticism in practice." "Judgment and Analysis" paved the way for extended criticism that involves criticism of the thought we find in the work of major creative writers: "tentative observations and local close criticism develop into a precise critical argument and the careful comprehensiveness of a written critique" (*LP,* 23). Leavis stresses that "[w]hat we have to get essential recognition for is that major creative writers are concerned with a necessary kind of thought" (*LP,* 20). It is thought, "antithetically remote from mathematics; it involves a consciousness of one's full human responsibility, purpose, and the whole range of human valuations" (*LP,* 21). It is thought reaching beyond that exemplified by Stanislav Andreski in *Social Sciences as Sorcery* though Leavis sees Andreski, because of his disinterested criticism of the social sciences, as "an ally who repays critical respect" (*LP,* 26). Leavis discusses the importance of words such as "value" and "standard" (*LP,* 27) for "English" as a discipline of thought. Also, he recommends Marjorie Grene's sixth chapter, "Facts and Values," of *The Knower and the Known* to "literary students to use as a main recourse for the acquiring of that knowledge of the development of philosophic thought from Descartes to Polanyi which is essential to their thinking" (*LP,* 29). For Leavis, *The Knower and the Known* is necessary reading in support of the conviction he shares with Marjorie Grene "that the Cartesian-Newtonian dualism must be exorcized from the Western mind" (*LP,* 31). In this respect, for Leavis, *The Knower and the Known* is far more useful than Bertrand Russell's *The History of Western Philosophy.*

In all our reading and discussion, it is essential, Leavis believes, to be continuously aware of "life," of "the Human World, the world created and renewed in day-by-day human collaboration through the ages" (*LP,* 34). Returning to "Judgment and Analysis," he argues that "[a]nalysis is a process of re-creation in response to the black marks on the pages. It is a more pondered following-through of the process of re-creation in response to the poet's words that any genuine and discussible reading of the poem must be" (*LP,* 35). Leavis argues here that "[a] judgment is personal and spontaneous or it is nothing" (*LP,* 35). He adds: "[t]he form of a judgment is 'This is so, isn't it?', the question asking for confirmation that the thing *is* so, but prepared for an answer in the form, 'Yes, but—,' the 'but' standing for corrections, refinements, precisions, amplifications" (*LP,* 35). Leavis goes on from this point to argue that "though the validity of a total inclusive judgment of a poem cannot be demonstrated, it is always possible in criticism to get beyond the mere assertion. The critical procedure is tactical; the critic, with his finger moving from this to that point in the text, aims at so ordering his particular judgments ('This is so, isn't it?') that, 'Yes" having in the succession of them almost inevitably come for answer, the rightness of the inclusive main judgment stands clear for the prompted recognition—it makes itself, needing no assertion" (*LP,* 35–36). He argues further (and this indicates that "creative critic" describes Leavis well) that "the very nature of the critical undertaking, which embodies a positive impulse, . . . has a creative purpose" (*LP,* 36). Leavis, restating the argument made in his Richmond Lecture that "[t]he poem is a product, and, in any experienced actual existence, a phenomenon, of human creativity" (*LP,* 36), concludes that "it belongs to the 'Third Realm'—the realm of that which is neither public in the ordinary sense nor merely private" (*LP,* 36).

Leavis also recommends two essays by Michael Polanyi, "The Logic of Tacit Inference" (1964) and "Sense-Giving and Sense-Reading" (1967), from *Knowing and Being* (1969), for reaching beyond "Cartesian dualism" (*LP,* 38), which Andreski, Leavis argues, appears to regard as unassailable. Polanyi argues that "what for philosophers is 'mind' is 'there' only in individual minds, and that an individual mind is always a person's and a person has a body and a history" (*LP,* 39). Mind and body are not separable. As Leavis puts it, "The dualism that has defeated so many epistemologies is eliminated here" (*LP*, 39). A major creative writer such as Blake or Dickens "tackles in sustained and unmistakably deliberate thought the basic unstatable that eludes the logic of Cartesian clarity—and of philosophic discourse too" (*LP*, 43). They reveal "the creativity of the artist as continuous with the general human creativity that, having created the human world we live in, keeps it renewed and real" (*LP*, 43–44). In the works of great creative writers such as Blake, Dickens, Conrad and Lawrence, Leavis sees a human responsibility that "is the manifest potency of life" (*LP*, 49). As creative critics accepting "English" as a discipline of thought, we develop a sense of the " 'living principle'—the principle implicit in the interplay between the living language and the creativity of individual genius" (*LP*, 49). Finally, Leavis recommends R. G. Collingwood's *The Idea of Nature,* and Lawrence's *Phoenix* as "an inexhaustible source of fresh insight, pregnant suggestion, and stimulus to thought" (*LP*, 54–55).

"Thought, Language, and Objectivity" concludes with Leavis taking issue with Ian Robinson over the latter's criticism in *The Survival of English* of Leavis's "belabouring Eliot with what amounts to jargon"[2] in his use of terms like *ahnung* and *nisus,* and what Robinson considers Leavis's exaggerated respect for Marjorie Grene's work. At the end of the section, Leavis defines the " 'living principle' " as "an apprehended totality of what, as registered in the language, has been won or established in immemorial human living" (*LP*, 68).

Section 2 of *The Living Principle,* "Judgment and Analysis" contains five subsections: (1) 'Thought' and Emotional Quality, (2) Imagery and Movement, (3) Reality and Sincerity, (4) Prose, and (5) *Antony and Cleopatra* and *All for Love.* " 'Thought' and Emotional Quality" is subtitled "Notes in the Analysis of Poetry." First, Leavis compares William Johnson Cory's "Heraclitus" and Walter Scott's "Proud Maisie" to show the emotional "disinterestedness" or "impersonality" in Scott's poem as opposed to Cory's "self-cherishing emotionality" (*LP*, 72). He continues by comparing Wordsworth's "A slumber did my spirit seal" and Tennyson's "Break, break, break." Leavis links Wordsworth's poem to Scott's when he comments, "No one can doubt that Wordsworth wrote his poem because of something profoundly and involuntarily suffered—suffered as a personal calamity, but the experience has been so impersonalised the effect, as much as that of *Proud Maisie,* is one of bare and disinterested presentment" (*LP*, 73). Scott's and Wordsworth's poems, as opposed to Cory's and Tennyson's, raise critical questions for Leavis of which he writes when he finds the latter "inferior" to the former poems: "'Inferior in kind'—by what standards? Here we come to the point at which literary criticism, as it must, enters overtly into questions of emotional hygiene and moral value—more generally (there seems no other adequate phrase), of spiritual health" (*LP,* 75).

Having considered two pairs of poems that "have presented strong and patent contrasts" (*LP,* 75), Leavis passes "to a comparison where the essential distinction is less obvious" (*LP,* 75), Lawrence's "Piano" and Tennyson's "Tears, idle tears. . . ." Here Leavis finds Lawrence's poem more complex and subtle than Tennyson's. Bringing Shelley into his discussion of Tennyson, Leavis censures poetry in which "'thought'" is separated from emotion: "one finds it a weakness in Shelley's poetry that feeling, as offered in it, depends for its due effect on a virtual abeyance in the thinking mind" (*LP,* 81). Following this interest, and differentiating between Victorian and Metaphysical poetry, Leavis compares Lionel Johnson's "By the Statue of King Charles at Charing Cross" and Andrew Marvell's "Horatian Ode on Cromwell's Return from Ireland." Leavis argues that Johnson's poem comes from "the 'soul,' that nineteenth-century region of specialized poetical experience where nothing has sharp definition and where effects of 'profundity' and 'intensity' depend upon a lulling of the mind" (*LP,* 84), whereas, in Marvell's poem, Leavis finds a "delicately ironic survey of contemporary history" and a "poised formal expression of statesmanlike wisdom" (*LP,* 87). Finally, Leavis considers the specious use of logic by Shelley in "Music, when soft voices die" in comparison to Blake's "The Sick Rose," in which he finds the "presence of 'thought'" (*LP,* 90).

"Imagery and Movement" is the second subsection of "Judgment and Analysis." In it Leavis first notes how discussions of the terms *image* and *imagery* are fraught with "two closely related fallacies: (i) the too ready assumption that images are visual, and (ii) the conception of metaphor as essentially simile with the 'like' or 'as' left out" (*LP,* 93). Leavis argues that more comes under "imagery" than visual effects—"tactual effects" and "evocations of different kinds of effort and movement" (*LP,* 93) are often involved as well. He then discusses Macbeth's speech in act 1, scene 7, "If it were done, when 'tis done . . . ," in part to show how the simile "pity, like a naked new-born babe" is "more-than-simile" (*LP,* 94). The speech, in fact, shows how important movement and tactual, as well as visual, effects are to what Leavis characterizes as "superb dramatic poetry" (*LP,* 94) that realizes "the perverse self-contradiction that makes Macbeth's inner state a tragic theme" (*LP,* 96). Besides, Leavis observes that "Shakespeare's poetry is the agent and vehicle of thought" (*LP,* 97). In this connection, he adds that "[t]he point to be stressed is that, whatever was gained by the triumph of 'clarity,' logic and Descartes, the gain was paid for by an immeasurable loss" (*LP,* 97). What was lost, in Leavis's view, was the Shakespearean use of language as a "vehicle of thought" (*LP,* 97). Discussing Samuel Johnson's inability to accept the true nature of Shakespeare's handling of language (though he often describes it well), Leavis adds: "Shakespeare compels one to recognize that language is essentially heuristic; that in major creative writers it does unprecedented things, advances the frontiers of the known, and discovers the new" (*LP,* 100). He concludes that "Shakespeare is concerned with meaning—meaning as language is concerned with it; and his art exemplifies supremely the truth that the fullest use of language is found in creative writing" (*LP,* 105).

Leavis goes on to describe the complexity of successful poetry, from which images cannot be pulled like plums from cake. "In reading a successful poem it is as if, with the kind of qualification intimated, one were living that particular action, situation or piece of life; the qualification representing the condition of the peculiar completeness and fineness of art" (*LP,* 111). Leavis completes his argument about successful poetry involving "movement" as much as "imagery" by comparing the two Wordsworth sonnets, "Calais Beach" and "Surprised by joy," in which the superiority of the latter to the former depends more upon "a striking difference in movement" than upon "imagery"—movement discoverable "in a sensitive reading-out" (*LP,* 114) of the two poems. In making the comparison, we come to realize that in "'Surprised by joy' we have deeply and finely experienced emotion poetically realized, the realization being manifested in a sensitive particularity, a delicate sureness of control in complex effects, and, in sum, a fineness of organization, such as could come only of a profoundly stirred sensibility in a gifted poet" (*LP,* 116). Leavis then introduces a third poem into the comparison, and shows how Wordsworth's "Upon Westminster Bridge," while appearing at first to express the "sunrise" emotion similar to the "sunset" emotion of "Calais Beach," is, in fact, a better, in part because a more carefully structured, poem. In conclusion, he offers a further simple example of the effective use of "movement" in Browning's "The gray sea and the long black land."

The discussion of "Imagery and Movement" is completed with a comparison of two four-line stanzas by A. E. Housman and eight lines by Edward Thomas. After discussing the handling of imagery and movement in each, Leavis concludes that "Housman's proffer of his imagery is simple and simple-minded: 'Here is poetical gold; take it! Here is radiant beauty; be moved.' What we are aware of from the first line in Edward Thomas's little poem is, along with the imagery, an attitude towards it; an attitude subtly conveyed and subtly developed" (*LP*, 124).

The third subsection of "Judgment and Analysis," "Reality and Sincerity" is another "exercise in critical comparison" (*LP*, 125) of Alexander Smith's "Barbara," Emily Brontë's "Cold in the earth," and Thomas Hardy's "After a Journey." As Leavis puts it, "The challenge was to establish an order of preference among these poems" (*LP*, 125). But, as he admits, only two of the poems were "seriously examined" (*LP*, 125). "Barbara" is quickly dismissed for having "all the vices that are to be feared when his theme is proposed, the theme of irreparable loss" (*LP*, 125). Leavis judges "Cold in the earth" "a notable achievement" in its "strong plangency" (*LP*, 127). However, the balance of his discussion is reserved for Hardy's "After a Journey," "a much rarer and finer thing, to be placed as a poetic achievement, decidedly higher" (*LP*, 127). What follows is one of the finest pieces of close critical analysis that Leavis wrote.

He first observes that Hardy's poem lacks the declamatory tone of Smith's and Brontë's poems, revealing instead a "convincing intimate naturalness" (*LP*, 128). The poem is "conversational" and "self-communing" (*LP*, 128). Words, that offend some readers, like "ejaculations" in line four, have "vivid precision" (*LP*, 129). Indeed, the poem is replete with "precisions of concrete realization, specificities, complexities" (*LP*, 129), "put side by side with Emily Brontë's, [it] is seen to have a great advantage in *reality*" (*LP*, 129). Only careful and detailed analysis can reveal this, and for Hardy's poem to have "an advantage in reality is to say (it will turn out) that it represents a profounder and completer sincerity" (*LP*, 129). Compared to Brontë's and Smith's poems, Hardy's reveals more "convincing concreteness of a presented situation" (*LP*, 130). Leavis then discusses the poem in detail, paying careful attention to its complexities of attitude and tone and to the effect of individual words. He attempts to capture the complexity of Hardy's response in an imagined summary: "The *real* for me, the focus of my affirmation, is the remembered realest thing, though to remember vividly is at the same time, inescapably, to embrace the utterness of loss" (*LP*, 133). What Leavis sees as the poem's "rare integrity appears in the way in which the two aspects, the affirmation and the void, affect us as equal presences in the poem" (*LP*, 133). In his ability to convey "both the emptiness and the quotidian ordinariness" (*LP*, 133), the sense of his late wife as living woman ("nut coloured hair, / And gray eyes, and rose-flush") and "thin ghost," Hardy offers "the purest fidelity, the sincerest tribute to the actual woman" (*LP*, 133). One of Leavis's greatest strengths as a critic lies in his ability to describe with sensitivity and precision what is developing in a poem line by line. He does not separate person and artist; intention and realization are, for him, closely related. However, he does not look only at local effects in the poem, but at the effect of the poem as a whole: "Hardy, with the subtlest and completest integrity, is intent on re-capturing what *can* be recaptured of that which, with all his being, he judges to have been the supreme experience of life, the realest thing, the centre of value and meaning" (*LP*, 134). Though Hardy now "fraily follows," he is "just the same as when / Our days were a joy, and our paths through flowers" (*LP*, 134).

The fourth subsection of "Judgment and Analysis" concerns "Prose." In it Leavis considers "dead metaphors," diagrammatic language, and the metaphoric life of prose. He disagrees with Herbert Read's rewriting of a passage about the Oxford Movement in *English Prose Style* because in reducing the metaphoric life of the passage Read has, in fact, distorted its thought. Leavis, then, discusses a passage from Swift's *The Tale of a Tub* as an example of "destructive creativity" (*LP*, 138). In its "astonishing play of imagery," Swift's "hatred of life, himself and the reader" (*LP*, 137) is revealed. Such hatred Leavis sees as a failure of intelligence: "it is not intelligence that prevails in Swift's intensely and incessantly communicated attitude to life" (*LP*, 138). Though he does not quote it, Leavis offers the fourth paragraph of chapter 15 of Edward Gibbon's *The Decline and Fall of the Roman Empire* as a contrast to the Swift passage, since it makes "a confident appeal to normative assumptions shared in common" (*LP*, 138). Leavis believes that "the intelligent study of creative literature entails the study of language in its fullest use" (*LP*, 139). His consideration of prose concludes with a comparison of passages by Conrad and Frederick Marryat. The Marryat passage, for Leavis, has a crude, obvious, and, therefore, insulting design on the reader (*LP*, 141), whereas in the Conrad passage, "creative art . . . is an exercise in the achieving of precision (a process that is at the same time the achieving of complete sincerity—the elimination of ego-interested distortion and all impure motives) in the recovery of a memory now implicitly judged—implicitly, for actual judgment can't be stated—to be, in a specific light, of high significance" (*LP*, 141). Though the Conrad passage "imposes itself, in its idiosyncratic livingness, as natural and unaffected modern English" (*LP*, 143), it has "a literature behind it—a great literature" (*LP*, 142). In Conrad's case "the English language that had adopted and naturalized him was the language not only of Shakespeare, but, in the not distant past, of Dickens" (*LP*, 143).

"Judgment and Analysis" ends with Leavis's comparison of passages from Shakespeare's *Antony and Cleopatra* and Dryden's *All For Love* in response to Bonamy Dobrée's argument that though " 'Shakespeare's play contains finer poetry than Dryden could ever write—as he would have been the first to admit—Dryden's has a more tragic effect' " (*LP*, 144). For Leavis, "[t]he superiority in poetry . . . makes it seem . . . absurd to compare the two plays in tragic effect" (*LP*, 144). Leavis sees even in the first 20 lines of *Antony and Cleopatra* "an immediately felt superiority in the life of the verse—superiority in concreteness, variety and sensitiveness—that leaves us with 'eloquence' instead of 'life' as the right word for Dryden's verse" (*LP*, 144–145). Where "Shakespeare's verse seems to enact its meaning, to do and to give rather than to talk about . . . Dryden's is merely descriptive eloquence" (*LP*, 146). Leavis supports this by analysis of the opening of Enobarbus's famous speech in act 2, scene 2: "The assonantal sequence, 'barge'—'burnish'd'—'burn'd,' is alien in spirit to Dryden's handling of the medium. . . . The effect is to give the metaphor 'burn'd' a vigour of sensuous realization that it wouldn't otherwise have had; the force of 'burn' is reflected back through 'burnish'd' (felt now as 'burning' too) upon 'barge,' so that the barge takes fire, as it were, before our eyes: we are much more than merely told that the barge 'burn'd' " (*LP*, 146–47). Shakespeare makes "language create and enact instead of merely saying and relating" (*LP*, 147). Leavis argues further that we can't imagine Dryden's Antony whistling in the marketplace or his Cleopatra hopping in the public street since "[h]is tragic *personae* exist only in a world of stage-postures; decorum gone, everything is gone" (*LP*, 151). In contrast, "Shakespeare's have a life corresponding to the life in the verse; the life in them is, in fact, the life of the verse" (*LP*, 151). For Leavis, Dryden in *All For Love* writes verse, where Shakespeare in *Antony and Cleopatra* is a dramatic poet. In Dryden's verse we do not find "the life of metaphor and imagery" that we find in Shakespeare's, rather "when we can put a finger on anything, [it] is almost invariably either a formal simile or a metaphor that is a simile with the 'like' or the 'as' left out" (*LP*, 151). Again, in contrast, "Shakespeare's metaphor is, characteristically, less simple, as well as less tidy, than one of Dryden's" (*LP*, 154). Metaphor, for Leavis, is "something more immediate, complex and organic than [the] neat illustrative correspondence" (*LP*, 154) we find in *All For Love*.

"Judgment and Analysis" may have begun as lectures and *Scrutiny* articles in the late 1940s and early 1950s, but in *The Living Principle* it serves the purpose of Leavis's creative criticism and shows how his early close criticism grows naturally into his later sense of the work of the great creative writers as providing significant thought about reality. "Judgment and Analysis" prepares the reader well for Leavis's hundred page analysis of Eliot's *Four Quartets*.

Leavis begins his analysis of *Four Quartets* by quoting the first 15 lines of "Burnt Norton." He shows how the opening 10 lines read like discursive prose. Then, at line 11, "Footfalls echo in the memory," there is a change. Leavis quotes D. W. Harding's account of "Burnt Norton" in *Scrutiny* volume 5, number 2 (September 1936), that "[h]ere most obviously the poetry is a linguistic achievement, in this case an achievement in the creation of concepts. . . . One could say, perhaps, that the poem takes the place of the ideas of 'regret' and 'eternity' " (*LP*, 158). Leavis finds Harding's commentary perceptive, with the reservation that "reality" might be a better word than "eternity" for what Eliot seeks. He quotes the lines:

> Go, said the bird, for the leaves were full of children,
> Hidden excitedly, containing laughter.
> Go, go, go, said the bird: human kind
> Cannot bear very much reality.
>
> (*Four Quartets*, 8)

And comments, "At last we get the word itself, 'reality'—the word that gives us the nature of the adult quest, though it doesn't give us the nature of the upshot, goal or answer; it takes the whole complex work to do that. 'Reality,' that is, serves perhaps better than 'eternity' as an index of the preoccupation that explains the peculiarity, the 'music,' of 'Burnt Norton' " (*LP*, 162–63). Leavis indicates that he "experienced a very decided arrest at 'human kind / Cannot bear very much reality,' divining that this was an intimation of something basic in Eliot's 'answer' that I couldn't endorse" (*LP*, 164).

Leavis proceeds by indicating that *music, dance,* and *pattern* are key words in "Burnt Norton" as throughout *Four Quartets*. He asks the reader to consider R. G. Collingwood's "The New Theory of Matter," section 3 of part 3 of *The Idea of Nature,* for an understanding of "the revolution in physics that took place in the 1920s, and . . . the conse-

quences for intelligent non-technical thought and the nature of the real"
(*LP*, 168). Leavis points out that "[t]he reality his [Eliot's] concern for
which explains the emphasis laid on 'pattern' and 'dance' in his music is,
in contradistinction to the physicist's, spiritual" (*LP*, 175). Further,
Leavis considers "'[t]he pressure of urgent misery and self-disgust'
[that] describes admirably the motive force that Harding, rightly (I
think), judges to have impelled Eliot to creativity" (*LP*, 171). It is this
"misery and self-disgust" that Leavis will argue later motivates Eliot's
denial of human creativity. For Leavis, creativity is the true end of
human endeavour. For Eliot, on the other hand, as Leavis argues, "the
really real . . . is the eternal" (*LP*, 177). The poem raises questions that
"compel," Leavis writes, "one to determine and verify one's own ultimate
beliefs, and I am sure already that my answers to those questions are not
Eliot's" (*LP*, 178). Leavis is disturbed that "Eliot insists on the unreality,
the unlivingness, of life in time" (*LP*, 179). For Leavis, Eliot's problem is
that though "[h]e registers his recoil from mechanistic determinism; . . .
in doing so he denies life's essential creativity, though committed to vin-
dicating by creative means his *ahnung* of a spiritual reality he posits as the
only escape" (*LP*, 181). Leavis adds, "In this self-contradiction, from
which there is, for him, no escape, Eliot is imprisoned; it defeats intelligence in him and imposes, as clairvoyance and spiritual courage, an
acceptance of defeat" (*LP*, 181).

Leavis sees Eliot as trapping himself in a Coriolanus-like *hubris* of
humility that means being locked in "selfhood" as opposed to attaining
"identity" (the terms are Blake's) that finds "the individual being as
the focal manifestation of creative life" (*LP*, 185). Leavis argues that "[t]he
magnificent first movement of 'Burnt Norton' has not, in exploring the
paradoxes—the succession, transcending subtleties—of time, disposed
of time. If life is real, then time is an essential constituent of reality; for
time would seem to be inescapably involved in life" (*LP*, 188). Leavis's
"seem" is significant here in relation to Eliot's effort to transcend time in
Four Quartets; Leavis should have used the word *is*, since he does not
appear to believe that time can be transcended, whereas Eliot does at
"the still point of the turning world." Whether or not time can be transcended, or in what way, is a subject for debate with Leavis's account of
Four Quartets and with the poem itself. His essential difference with Eliot
emerges completely when he speaks of Eliot as "a divided man" with a
"gift for an equivocal subtlety of formulation" "that enabled him, in
writing (for example) an obituary of Robert Bridges, to satisfy the insti-

tutionalist *bien-pensants* while making the undisturbed dismissive judgment plain to readers like myself, who knew that Eliot's view of the deceased Laureate as a poet coincided with my own" (*LP*, 189). This trait in Eliot, Leavis argues, "went very deep. It went down to the core of the centrally divided inner being, and the attendant lack of courage in the face of life" (*LP*, 189). This, for Leavis, can't have anything but a severely limiting effect upon Eliot's poetry, and so, for Leavis, the transcendence proposed in "Burnt Norton" remains unachieved despite "the magnificent first movement" (*LP*, 188).

As with "Burnt Norton," Leavis is impressed by the opening of "East Coker." "And yet Eliot is a major poet: one's certainty of that is (if it could be supposed to have wavered) decisively renewed by the opening movement of 'East Coker' " (*LP*, 192):

> Now the light falls
> Across the open field, leaving the deep lane
> Shuttered with branches, dark in the afternoon,
> Where you lean against a bank while a van passes,
> And the deep lane insists on the direction
> Into the village, in the electric heat
> Hypnotised.
>
> (*Four Quartets*, 15)

Leavis comments on this passage that "[t]he major quality of the poet is manifest in the vivid completeness of the immediacy" (*LP*, 193). However, Leavis finds "a most gravely disabling ignorance" in the way Eliot "presents the country-folk of pre-industrial England" (*LP*, 195). As Leavis points out, the people who Eliot caricatures "created the English language—robust, supple, humanly sensitive and illimitably responsive and receptive—and made possible in due course Shakespeare, Dickens and the poet of *Four Quartets*" (*LP*, 196–97). Leavis describes the effect that Eliot's "East Coker" has on him: "He [Eliot] compels one, as a genius can, to the kind of disagreement that, positively, is a sharpening of one's power to perceive and to realize, and a strengthening of one's thought, conviction and resolution" (*LP*, 202). He argues that Eliot's "human kind / Cannot bear very much reality" "soon turns out to involve an essential nihilism," "for, the reality that Eliot seeks to apprehend being spiritual must be thought of as the absolutely 'other'—the antithetically and excludingly non-human" (*LP*, 203). Though Leavis believes that Eliot suffers from "inner conflict bred by irremediable self-division" (*LP,* 203), his importance to us lies in "his using a major poet's command of the English language to bring home to us the spiritual philistinism of our civilization" (*LP,* 205).

Leavis argues that:

> the nature of the drive behind *Four Quartets* is given in "The Hollow Men." The urgent question is: "What *can* I affirm?" It commits him to the profoundest and completest sincerity he can achieve, and his poetic technique, with its astonishing diversities of originality, is a technique for that. One way of intimating the rare kind of value the poem has for us is to say that it provides us with an incomparable study of what, in its most serious use, is meant by "sincerity"—a word we cannot do without. (*LP,* 209)

He elaborates the questions that Eliot asks in *Four Quartets*: "What can I with certainty affirm? By what tests, what tactical approaches, do I arrive at my certitude and assure myself that it is valid and inescapable?" (*LP,* 210). Leavis believes that "sincerity (in the profoundest and completest sense . . . is what the study of *Four Quartets* should illuminate and lead us to ponder)" (*LP,* 211). Despite his reservations about "East Coker" and *Four Quartets* as a whole, Leavis believes that, in the last verse paragraph of "East Coker," Eliot "is unequivocally a great poet again" (*LP,* 215–16).

Likewise, Leavis finds the opening of "The Dry Salvages" "in its nervous flexibility . . . a magnificent piece of Eliotic poetry" (*LP,* 216). He thinks that the first movement of the quartet could stand as a poem by itself. After the first movement, though, Leavis finds Eliot expressing a "fear of death which is a fear of life; the 'resentment' felt at failing powers before it is plausible to represent them as failing; the insecurity that, calling itself pride, takes Coriolanus ('broken') for its symbol" (*LP,* 221). Leavis sees a "close relation between Eliot's denial of human creativity and his attitude to time" (*LP,* 222). He does not think that Eliot succeeds in *Four Quartets* in making his "personal affirmation" fully convincing to the reader. Part of the problem, in Leavis's view, is that the word *pattern,* as Eliot uses it in the poem, contains "no thought that will bear scrutiny—no thought that really plays its ostensible part in a total cogency" (*LP,* 223). Leavis thinks that Eliot has an insufficient sense of the creative activity implied in the word *pattern.* Eliot, in Leavis's view, seems unwilling to accept that "[s]ince life is process, time is of its reality" (*LP,* 225).

Leavis argues that "*Four Quartets* repays a closely critical yet sympathetic study. The defeated genius *is* a genius, and the creative power is inseparable from the significance of the defeat. Eliot was a victim of our civilization. We all suffer from the malady that afflicts it, and the power with which he makes us recognize the malady and feel it ('Cry what shall I cry?') for what it is, establishes him as a great poet of our time, one whose work has the closest relevance to our basic problems" (*LP*, 228). What troubles Leavis is Eliot's divided attitude to human creativity and his inability to establish his affirmation as more than merely personal. Leavis believes that, in Eliot's case, his "reaction to the sickness of humanity is potent, and we may call it diagnostic, but his constructive thought is weak; it lacks the necessary impersonality. The thinker is immersed in his own plight" (*LP*, 232). He compares Eliot's and R. G. Collingwood's idea of the word *pattern,* much to the advantage of Collingwood as expressed in his *The Idea of Nature.* Also, he invokes Michael Polanyi's anti-Cartesian—and anti-Eliotic—understanding in "The Logic of Tacit Inference," that "All thought is incarnate: it lives by the body and by the favour of society. But it is not *thought* unless it strives for truth, a striving which leaves it free to act on its own responsibility, with universal intent" (qtd. in *LP*, 233). Blake, with his distinction between "selfhood" and "identity," is also noted as having, for Leavis, the right sense of human responsibility. Polanyi and Blake, Leavis argues, agree that discovery involves creativity (*LP*, 234). For Leavis, Blake and Polanyi are able to discover "the real," whereas "[t]he 'humility' defined and evoked in *Four Quartets* is the refusal of responsibility" (*LP*, 235).

Leavis criticizes Eliot for his too-ready dismissal of evolutionary development, of the work, for example, of Alexander, Alfred North Whitehead and Collingwood. As Leavis puts it, "In the work of these distinguished minds process, development and the telic are *of* the vital principle informing the thought; they are in and of the thought's creativity—a creativity that, in various ways, is nourished by a close acquaintance with the achievements of modern science" (*LP*, 235). Despite the achievement of *Four Quartets,* Leavis fears that "the Eliotic enterprise, . . . is one, not of human responsibility, but of human abjectness" (*LP*, 238). Leavis is concerned throughout to note "the inner contradiction, the dividedness, that plays an inseparable part in the paradoxical Eliotic creativity" (*LP*, 240). Eliot, in *Four Quartets,* seems to Leavis to express "the steady aim of realizing in his own person the abject nullity of human kind ('that which is only living can only die')" (*LP*, 245). For these reasons the affirmation that Eliot makes at the close of "The Dry Salvages" is, for Leavis, problematic: "Eliot's affirmation is not coercively entailed in the way he supposes; there is about it none of the inevitability of issue out of what has gone before that he invites us to be impressed by" (*LP*, 248). For Leavis, then, the affirmation that Eliot makes at the conclusion of "The Dry Salvages" fails to gain a general or universal validity and remains, instead, limitingly personal.

Commenting on "Little Gidding," Leavis finds a relaxed quality in most of it. The verse lacks metaphorical life when compared to the superior section of terza rima in the second movement of the quartet. He thinks the terza rima section as strong as anything in Eliot's canon and finds "the sinister reality of bombed London . . . wonderfully evoked" (*LP*, 250). However, Leavis remains troubled by "Eliot's insistence on humanity's utter abjectness and nullity and on the supremely Real as the completely Other" (*LP*, 255). He disagrees sharply with D. W. Harding's account of "Little Gidding" in *Experience into Words*, finding that his "uncritically sympathetic approach makes him *essentially* unfair to Eliot" (*LP*, 257). In his discussion, Leavis quotes the passage from the terza rima section in which Eliot encounters "The eyes of a familiar compound ghost / Both intimate and unidentifiable." Instantly, revealing the dividedness that Leavis analyzed, the poet "assume[s] a double part" (*LP*, 259). Even so, Leavis argues that Eliot comes close "to achieve the full self-recognition that, ordinarily, something precludes. What that 'something' is he comes nearer to recognizing with due courage in this creatively strongest part of 'Little Gidding' than anywhere else in his work" (*LP*, 259). Here, Leavis believes that Eliot comes close to facing his own sense of shame:

> the shame
> Of motives late revealed, and the awareness
> Of things ill done and done to others' harm
> Which once you took for exercise of virtue.
> (*Four Quartets*, 39–40)

This shame, Leavis argues, is close to that felt by Harry, the protagonist of *The Family Reunion*, "through whom Eliot is clearly exploring, and endeavouring to master, a problem that he himself is troubled by, [who] suffers the torments of a consciousness of guilt that he can't explain" (*LP*, 262). Through further comparison with *The Family Reunion*, Leavis adduces that "[t]he sin recognized in the truly strong section of 'Little Gidding' as requiring expiation is a sin against life" (*LP,* 263).

Leavis concludes his discussion of *Four Quartets* by quoting D. W. Harding's commentary on the fourth section of "Little Gidding," which he thinks is "how Eliot's own commentary might have run" (*LP,* 264):

> the fourth section is a forceful passage, close-knit with rime and incisive. Its theme is the terrifying fierceness of the pentecostal experience, the dove bringing fire. This is not the fire of expiation, such as the humanist had to suffer. It is the consuming experience of love, the surrender to a spiritual principle beyond us, and the only alternative to consuming ourselves with the miserable fires of sin and error. This pentecostal ordeal must be met before the blinding promise seen in "midwinter spring" can be accepted. (qtd. in *LP,* 264)

Leavis cannot accept Harding's account. Though Eliot was the poet during and immediately after World War I who "altered expression," and though Leavis finds magnificent poetry in *Four Quartets* and regards it as Eliot's major achievement, he nevertheless sees Eliot as a "case" who reveals a divided attitude toward human creativity.

In contrast, Leavis regards D. H. Lawrence—about whom he wrote his last book, *Thought, Words, and Creativity: Art and Thought in Lawrence* (1976), published when he was 81—as the major writer who succeeds where Eliot fails. Lawrence, for Leavis, represents life and a full realization of human creativity. Also, he believes that Lawrence's work is significant as thought. Where Eliot is a symptom of the modern disease, Lawrence represents the cure. Part of the cure lies in what Leavis regards as a creative attitude to human relationship as indicated in the book's third epigraph, a quotation from Lawrence himself: "Man or woman, each is a flow, a flowing life. And without one another, we can't flow, just as a river cannot flow without banks. A woman is one bank of the river of my life, and the world is the other."[3]

In his Preface, Leavis indicates that he wishes to consider the "embracing organic totality of Lawrence's thought" (*TWC,* 9). For the sake of economy of argument, he chooses to consider, in order, four works of Lawrence's: *The Plumed Serpent, Women in Love, The Captain's Doll,* and *The Rainbow.* Leavis does not share Lawrence's view of *The Plumed Serpent* as "[m]y most important thing so far" (qtd. in *TWC,* 34). Rather, he indicates that he wishes to consider it "as a foil to *Women in Love,* which I am not alone in judging the greatest and most important of his novels" (*TWC,* 9–10). He then states that he has chosen to discuss one of Lawrence's "supreme *nouvelles*" (*TWC*, 10), *The Captain's Doll*, rather than the other, *St. Mawr*, because it better suits his argument about Lawrence's thought. He indicates that he will close with a discussion of *The Rainbow*'s paradox, which helps us to understand "the element of paradox at the heart of *Women in Love*; paradox that is inseparable from [the] greatness" of that "self-sufficient great novel" (*TWC*, 11). Leavis concludes his Preface by quoting Lawrence again, this time the epigraph from *The Living Principle*: "It is no use trying merely to modify present forms. The whole great form of our era will have to go. And nothing will really send it down but the new shoots of life springing up and slowly bursting the foundations. And one can do nothing but fight tooth and nail to defend the new shoots of life from being crushed out, and let them grow" (qtd. in *TWC*, 12–13). For Leavis, "[t]he faith that we must keep alive is that what we stand for *are* the living shoots. Lawrence—and not the less for what I have called the 'paradox'—is a potent inspiration and source of strength to that end" (*TWC*, 13). Briefly, the paradox that Leavis identifies in Lawrence is something very different from the dividedness he sees in Eliot. Lawrence loved the traditional life he dramatizes in *The Rainbow* but at the same time he was part of the Eastwood intelligentsia that came with industrialism. Lawrence was not nostalgic; he knew that life involved change and that, properly used, the machine could free human beings for more creative pursuits than repetitive work.

Leavis's first chapter, "Thought, Words, and Creativity," draws an immediate distinction between Eliot and Lawrence. Eliot in *The Criterion* found Lawrence "incapable of what is ordinarily called thinking" (qtd. in *TWC*, 15). Eliot, Leavis argues, was himself incapable of recognizing the "astonishing powers, so profound and compelling, of original thought in Lawrence" (*TWC*, 15). As Leavis points out, "Eliot was not alone in *not* being compelled" by "the wonder and significance" of Lawrence's creativity (*TWC*, 15). Leavis sees Lawrence's creativity in his criticism and Lawrence's criticism as superior to Eliot's. For Leavis, Eliot's best criticism was directly related to his creative practice and was written early in his career. Leavis continues with a sharp attack on Eliot's Francophilia and "famous doctrine of impersonality" (*TWC*, 16–17). He reiterates his view of *Four Quartets*, which he regards as Eliot's "magnum opus," though it "is devoted to sustained exploratory thought, the thought frustrates itself by reason of the contradiction at its heart" (*TWC*, 17). Leavis relates Eliot's denial of "human creativity" to the killing of "the very idea of creativity" by "our all-conquering civilization" (*TWC*, 18).

He argues that all we are now interested in is "economic growth" and a "rising standard of living" (*TWC*, 18).

For Leavis, in contrast to Eliot, Lawrence's "life-as-intelligence" is "at the same time an exaltation of creative life, and inseparable from an acceptance of responsibility as inhering, necessarily, in the human individual's self-gathered, delicately, intent and unanalysably intuitive wholeness" (*TWC*, 19). Leavis then proposes to address Lawrence's "thought" with three "propositions or constations" in mind:

(1) There could be no developed thought of the most important kind without language.

(2) Our language is English, which has a great literature, so that one had better say: the completest use of the English language is to be found in major creative works.

(3) A major creative writer *knows* that in composing and writing a major creative work his concern is to refine and develop his profounder thought about life (the concluding three-word phrase unambiguously eliminates mathematics). (*TWC*, 20)

Within Lawrence, Leavis finds works that can be read "as completely achieved art" (*TWC*, 20) such as *Women in Love*, "The Fox," and "The Captain's Doll," as well as works that "unmistakably [offer] us something else" (*TWC*, 20) like "The Crown," *Study of Thomas Hardy*, and *Psychoanalysis and the Unconscious*. In the last of these, Leavis argues, "Lawrence's aim is to enforce his criticism of our civilization and culture by showing what the human individual is in his wholeness, his living integrity as the actual presence of life, must be realized to be" (*TWC*, 21). *Psychoanalysis and the Unconscious* is, in part, a criticism of Freud's "incest-doctrine" (*TWC*, 21). In works like this, Leavis argues, the reader is more conscious of Lawrence as expositor than in the novels and stories in which the reader is "not kept actively aware of [Lawrence] as a personal voice expounding or aiming to evoke" (*TWC*, 22). At the same time, both *Women in Love* and *Psychoanalysis and the Unconscious*, Leavis believes, "derive in perfect directness from the one vital intelligence and the one achieved wholeness of individual being" (*TWC*, 22). Leavis indicates that Lawrence himself thought "it was the greatest pity in the world, when philosophy and fiction got split" (*TWC*, 22), because the novel has become "sloppy" and "abstract-dry" (*TWC*, 22–23). Lawrence believes that "[t]he two should come together again—in the novel" (qtd. in *TWC*, 23).

Leavis sees Lawrence as challenging the limited conceptions of philosophy and thought we find in *"la clarté* and *la logique"* (*TWC,* 23). "'Logic,' says Lawrence, 'is far too coarse to make the subtle distinctions life demands'" (*TWC,* 23). In Lawrence's thought, Leavis argues, "vital mental consciousness is neither apart in the individual human being, separated off, nor dominating, initiating and controlling" (*TWC,* 23). Both in Lawrence's novels and in works like *Psychoanalysis and the Unconscious,* Leavis finds "a searching of experience in the concrete 'knowledge,' not only of the desired individual wholeness, but of what 'spontaneity' means and, with it, 'responsibility'" (*TWC,* 26). Leavis argues that, in Lawrence's case, "the fictively imaginative achieved art and the expository modes, springing from the one root, are vitalized by the one sap, and that there can be no question of a genetic or dynamic priority to be assigned to either of them. Nevertheless it is plain that he sees himself primarily as a novelist" (*TWC,* 28). Also, though, Leavis believes that Lawrence is "as great a critic as there has ever been" (*TWC,* 32). For Leavis, "Lawrence the great novelist and critic *is* the great psychologist" (*TWC,* 32).

In the second chapter of his study, Leavis faces the question of how Lawrence could have regarded *The Plumed Serpent,* rather than *Women in Love,* as his "most important thing so far." Though *The Plumed Serpent* is 15,000 words shorter than *Women in Love,* Leavis notes that he has always found it "slow-going" (*TWC,* 51). Nevertheless, in Lawrence's attempt to recover religion through his experience of Mexico, Leavis believes that "*The Plumed Serpent,* as thought, is neither irrelevant nor redundant in relation to those basic works, *Psychoanalysis and the Unconscious, Study of Thomas Hardy,* and *Introduction to these Paintings"* (*TWC,* 57). However, he finds that "*Women in Love,* which is inclusive, cogent and concrete in the treatment of the complex Laurentian theme, is a better work of art than *The Plumed Serpent,* and the superiority as art is superiority as thought—which amounts to a greater cogency" (*TWC,* 58). In this connection, in *The Plumed Serpent* he finds Kate Leslie "the one character of major intrinsic interest, the one major personal value" (*TWC,* 58) in the novel. Leavis argues that Kate Leslie, like Mrs. Witt in *St. Mawr,* "feels the void and can't forget the unanswerable 'What for?—what ultimately for?'" (*TWC,* 59). For Leavis, the problem with *The Plumed Serpent* is that "Lawrence can, 'in imagination,' solve the Ursula-Birkin problem very easily in Mexico—so easily that the show of its being dealt with in *The Plumed Serpent* as inseparable from the theme of that book can't be taken at all seriously" (*TWC,* 60). Leavis argues, in conclusion, that while Lawrence's imagination is usually "concerned intensely for the real" (*TWC*, 60), in *The Plumed Serpent* there is an "element of *un*realism inescapably entailed in the theme" (*TWC*, 60) of the novel. Leavis poses the question, "Is it really credible that in actuality Ramón's drive could have had as much success as the novel represents it as having?" (*TWC*, 61). *Women in Love* dramatizes "the Ursula-Birkin problem" more successfully than *The Plumed Serpent*.

Women in Love, which Leavis discusses in chapter 3, is more successful than *The Plumed Serpent*, because after the opening of the novel "it is impossible to suppose that in *Women in Love* the Laurentian emphasis on the vitally essential but terribly difficult relation between the fully individual man and the fully individual woman is going to be external and marginal to some ostensibly more embracing theme, as it *is* in *The Plumed Serpent*" (*TWC*, 63). In realizing the relations between men and women in *Women in Love*, Lawrence reveals, for Leavis, that his "genius is that of a supremely great novelist—which is to say that his art is thought and his thought art" (*TWC*, 64). Leavis argues that Lawrence's "thought and novelistic art" are "one (a truth potently exemplified in the opening chapter)" (*TWC*, 66). In Lawrence's case, Leavis believes, that "[l]ike that of all great creative writers, his creativity manifests itself in new shades of suggestion, new felicities of force, got out of the common language—in (we feel) an inspired way, rather than by calculating intention" (*TWC*, 67). Besides, Lawrence is concerned with truth and with the real: "I think we may fairly say that Lawrence intends us to identify with his own Ursula's attitude and her conclusion: 'The world of art is only the truth about the real world, that's all . . .'" (*TWC*, 77).

With his art-which-is-thought, Lawrence is able to explore the different forms of egoism in Thomas and Gerald Crich, representative nineteenth- and twentieth-century capitalists, but also fully dramatized individuals. Beyond such explorations as these, Lawrence addresses, as Leavis indicates, "'What ultimately for?' and the problem of love; or rather, the problem of finding the right answers, the humanly most satisfying answers, to serious self-questioning about the relations between individual women and individual men" (*TWC*, 81–82). The "interplay" of relations between Birkin and Ursula, Gerald and Gudrun, Leavis suggests, presents them dramatically as significant thought about relationships between men and women. As well as issues of relationship, Lawrence, Leavis notes, considers the nature of individuality, individual integrity, and the need to draw creative inspiration from sources beyond the self. The Gerald-Gudrun relationship fails, but, as Leavis concludes,

"Ursula . . . so different from Gudrun, knew that she had for husband a man whose individual life was open to the deep source, to the unknown, and who had his part in the creativity that kept civilization rooted and changing—that is alive. But he couldn't have been that without her" (*TWC*, 91).

In his fourth chapter, Leavis discusses Lawrence's novella "The Captain's Doll." He begins by considering the importance of Lawrence's dictum, " 'Nothing is important but life' " (*TWC*, 92). As Leavis himself puts it in relation to creativity *and* criticism, " 'Life' *Is* a Necessary Word."[4] He notes that "the complex totality of *Women in Love* is needed to convey the superlative force and nuance, the supreme value, the word 'life' has for [Lawrence's] creative thought" (*TWC*, 94). In "The Captain's Doll," he finds that "the treatment of the love-theme . . . is equally a treatment of the life-theme" (*TWC*, 94), as indeed it is in *Women in Love,* which is, for Leavis, "the great Laurentian inquest into our civilization and what menaces it—the drive that impels it to self-destruction" (*TWC*, 94). In "The Captain's Doll" the themes of love and life are treated in a less complex way, though "the tale is amply enough invested with a complexity of its own, and is full of very relevant felicities" (*TWC*, 94). Leavis finds Lawrence's ". . . Love was once a Little Boy" from *Phoenix II* relevant to "The Captain's Doll," especially the quotation "Hate is not the opposite of love. The real opposite of love is individuality. We live in the age of individuality, we call ourselves the servants of love. That is to say, we enact a perpetual paradox" (qtd. in *TWC*, 95). In this quotation, Leavis argues, "We have . . . what might be said to be a general statement of the problem that faces the Captain and Hannele in 'The Captain's Doll' " (*TWC*, 95). From here, Leavis proceeds to discuss the shifting relations between the Captain and Hannele. He notes that "[h]ere we have the theme of the tale; the problem to which the answer, the complex answer, is arrived at by shared ordeal, or lived experience gone through between Hannele and the Captain" (*TWC*, 101).

The difference between the doll and the Captain, Hannele discovers, is that "[t]he Captain's mystery is so potent because the life in him flows with unusual freedom from the source or well-head, so that he has the responsibility of one who is exquisitely sensitive to the unknown, and, being in delicate touch with the dark pregnancy, is capable of wonder—and of growth; that is, new livingness, which issues from the as yet unknown" (*TWC*, 107). Hannele comes to recognize that in making a doll of the Captain she has denied his changing "life"—the necessary word for Lawrence and for Leavis. This is why she wishes to burn the still life in which the doll is represented. The tale's conflict between love and individuality is resolved, as Leavis notes, by "the pair's becoming— the pair they essentially are or are meant to be—formally and really husband and wife" (*TWC*, 119). Leavis elaborates: "They are intimate with a reality far more real than the intimacy of a pair of lovers intoxicated with the passion of adoring love" (*TWC*, 119). As Leavis adds, "Hannele married won't be the less Hannele" (*TWC*, 121).

Leavis ends his analysis of "The Captain's Doll" with a modest comment that reveals the extent of his ability to offer us insight into Lawrence's "art and thought" or art-as-thought. "It is perhaps proper to insist after such an exercise, of which I am all too conscious of the clumsiness, that I have not been offering to define any thought that is *behind* the novel-long tale. The tale itself *is* the thought; my clumsy commentary is meant as an aid to perceiving that the delicate perfection of Lawrence's art-speech can be duly appreciated only as the precision and completeness of the thinking" (*TWC*, 121).

In chapter 5, Leavis discusses *The Rainbow*. He argues that whereas "*Women in Love* is, of its nature, dynamic, and, as such, straining urgently, and very responsive to impulsions of change, it is nevertheless a present—England now. The distinctive offer of *The Rainbow* is to render development concretely—the complex change from generation to generation and the interweaving of the generations" (*TWC*, 125). Leavis observes that though the two books are markedly different in style, "the implicit criteria, and something characteristic of the method of *Women in Love*, are what have been worked out in the writing of *The Rainbow*" (*TWC*, 125). He notes that Skrebensky poses the same kind of problem for Ursula in *The Rainbow* that Gerald poses for Gudrun in *Women in Love*: "Gudrun is attracted by Gerald Crich's male beauty and the masterfulness of his organizing talent and will; and then repelled by the emptiness of his intrinsic being—just as Ursula had been by Skrebensky's conventional nullity—as a centre of life" (*TWC*, 130–31).

Leavis also discusses the meaning of the novel's title. "The Laurentian rainbow meant faith-in-life overhung by frightening menace—menace yoked, for the 'conscious,' with a paradoxical contradiction. The novel offers to bring before us the immediate past of the England of *Women in Love*" (*TWC*, 137). Leavis adds, later, "that the naïve rainbow-symbol as [Lawrence] subtilized it, making it paradoxical, is valid for us" (*TWC*, 145). He concludes that Lawrence, with his paradoxical rainbow, dares "to postulate that human life will go on. I felt the courage grow in me as

I met more and more people who shared my conviction about him and the nature of his genius: he has readers who understand him" (*TWC*, 145). Perhaps Leavis's most important work as a literary critic has been his interpreting and arguing for the importance of Lawrence. At the end of his chapter on *The Rainbow*, Leavis associates the growing number of intelligent readers of Lawrence with the necessary re-creation of an educated public.

Leavis ends *Thought, Words, and Creativity* with a sixth chapter, called "Further Considerations." In it he mentions Lawrence's "early long 'Study of Thomas Hardy' which he never published (it is a preliminary sustained self-exploration, carried out arduously and comprehensively, to establish for himself what he believes and where he stands)" (*TWC*, 150). From it Leavis quotes a passage in praise of the machine's liberating us from routine drudgery so that we can be and use our time creatively. For Leavis, Lawrence was a vital example of genius, "of radiant potency—of life that irradiates people in whom the creativity is less powerful" (*TWC*, 156). Lawrence, in Leavis's judgment, possessed a "power of spontaneous interest (which was itself creative) was always growing and always open to the new" (*TWC*, 153). He discusses the relationship between Henry and March in "The Fox" as "comparable in significance to the successful close of Birkin's courtship of Ursula" (*TWC*, 155). These characters as Lawrence dramatizes them have what Leavis describes as "difference that is essential to life" (*TWC*, 156). For Leavis, finally, Lawrence offers us "the incitement, which is irresistible, of the life-courage in the product of his creativity, and that makes it inevitable for us to carry on the creative effort with all our intelligence, courage and resource. Who can be sure? Logic and automatism, impossible as it now seems, may yet be robbed of their final victory; the decisively new and unforeseen may yet reward us" (*TWC*, 156). Right to the end Leavis, with Lawrence's help, maintained his hope.

Chapter Seven
Conclusion: Literature and Culture

F. R. Leavis devoted his life to literary criticism. He showed students and common readers what it meant to take literature seriously. Taken seriously, in the way that Leavis took it, the study of great works of literature could, and did, change lives. Already interested in poetry and contemporary writing, such as the stories of D. H. Lawrence, before going to World War I, through which he carried the World's Classics edition of Milton's poems, Leavis changed from History to English on completing part one of the History Tripos in 1919. In changing to English he entered what would come to be known as Cambridge English. He emerged as its most distinguished representative.

Cambridge English in the 1920s combined two important elements: the close reading of literary works championed by Mansfield D. Forbes and I. A. Richards (Leavis attended their lecture series in Practical Criticism several times) and the study of literature in its cultural context associated with H. Munro Chadwick. These elements Leavis combined powerfully in his own criticism. It is significant that his Ph.D. thesis written for Sir Arthur Quiller-Couch, himself a journalist and novelist, should have concerned "The Relationship of Journalism to Literature: Studied in the Rise and Earlier Development of the Press in England." Also, Leavis's first two pamphlets, published in 1930, reflect his related interests in literature and culture. In the first pamphlet, *Mass Civilisation and Minority Culture,* he argued for the need for an educated minority to defend culture against the leveling-down process of mass civilization. *D. H. Lawrence,* the second, concerned the contemporary writer best qualified, in Leavis's view, to resist mass civilization in the name of living literature. Leavis continued to move readily between these two concerns (literature and culture), between which he saw little separation. For Leavis, literature must be dynamically, as well as organically, related to culture. Thus, his best known early study, *New Bearings in English Poetry,* was subtitled *A Study of the Contemporary Situation.* This movement between detailed analyses of literature and discussions of literature's cultural relation continued throughout Leavis's career.

115

In 1932, the same year in which he published *New Bearings in English Poetry,* Leavis published *How to Teach Reading: A Primer for Ezra Pound.* While agreeing with Pound about literature's social importance, Leavis questioned Pound's judgment of individual writers as well as Pound's attempt to discuss technique independent of content and individual works independent of the tradition from which they emerged. Also at this time, he was closely involved with the launching of *Scrutiny* which, with the help of Q. D. Leavis, he sustained for 20 years. *Scrutiny* revealed Leavis's continuous concern with literature in its cultural context. The publication, the following year, of *For Continuity* and *Culture and Environment: The Training of Critical Awareness* again revealed the nature of Leavis's interest in the relationship between literature and society. The subtitle of *Culture and Environment* makes it plain that Leavis found "critical awareness" essential in dealing with the survival of a vital culture in the environment of mass civilization. *Revaluation: Tradition and Development in English Poetry* (1936), while discovering "new bearings" in the tradition of English poetry, also stressed the importance of continuity in the development of a vital, contemporary poetry. Though ending with discussion of Keats, *Revaluation* was clearly related to *New Bearings in English Poetry,* in which, in preparing to discuss the moderns, Leavis had already dealt with Victorian poetry.

During World War II, Leavis's critical attention moved to the novel and to educational issues. *Education and the University: A Sketch for an "English School"* appeared in 1943 and *The Great Tradition: George Eliot, Henry James, and Joseph Conrad* in 1948. At the same time, he was developing his idea of the "novel as a dramatic poem" in articles in *Scrutiny.* In 1952, *The Common Pursuit,* thought by many to be Leavis's finest selection of essays, appeared. Characteristically, in this volume Leavis deals with Eliot's retraction over Milton, with problems in Hopkins's scholarship, with Swift's self-hatred, with Pope's ability to make satire into major poetry, with Johnson as poet, with Shakespearean tragedy, *Measure for Measure,* and the criticism of Shakespeare's last plays, with literature and society, literary criticism and philosophy, and with John Bunyan, Henry James, Eliot, Lawrence, and Bloomsbury. It is revealing to note how the volume begins and ends in critical engagement with Eliot. Leavis is often described as a controversialist; his literary and social criticism is never less than fully engaged. *D. H. Lawrence: Novelist* was published in 1955, a distillation of Leavis's critical response to Lawrence over 30 years.

With retirement, in 1962, Leavis was able to continue his literary and social polemics in a series of public lectures. This began with his famous Richmond Lecture, "Two Cultures? The Significance of C. P. Snow," and continued with his Chichele lecture at Oxford on *Little Dorrit,* the culmination of his revaluation of Dickens, which appeared in *Dickens the Novelist* (1970), written together with Q. D. Leavis. A follow-up to the Richmond Lecture, "Luddites? *or* There is Only One Culture," was delivered in the United States and gathered along with essays on Eliot and Yeats and with Q. D. Leavis's "A Fresh Approach to *Wuthering Heights*" in *Lectures in America* (1969). In the same year, Leavis's Clark Lectures (given at Trinity College, Cambridge, in 1967) appeared as *English Literature in Our Time and the University.* Two of Leavis's titles, once again, indicate the nature of his interest in the educational and cultural context of literature, "Literature and the University: The Wrong Question" and "Why *Four Quartets* Matters in a Technologico-Benthamite Age." Two years earlier, Chatto and Windus had published a selection of Leavis's essays, mainly on the novel and criticism, as *"Anna Karenina" and Other Essays,* but even there the final essay, "The Orthodoxy of Enlightenment," indicates Leavis's commitment to challenging the "Technologico-Benthamite Age," which was his unremitting focus in his gathering of postretirement lectures, *Nor Shall My Sword: Discourses on Pluralism, Compassion, and Social Hope* (1972).

In his Clark Lectures Leavis saw Lawrence as the "necessary opposite" to Eliot. This contrast between the century's greatest novelist and greatest poet became the subject of Leavis's last two books. In *The Living Principle: "English" As a Discipline of Thought* (1975), Leavis undertook a sustained analysis of *Four Quartets* in which he criticizes Eliot's failure to believe sufficiently in human creativity. Finally, in *Thought, Words, and Creativity: Art and Thought in Lawrence* (1976), Lawrence emerges, once more, as the "necessary opposite" to Eliot. Leavis saw Lawrence's belief in human creativity as essential to the survival of English literature and culture.

Leavis agreed with Eliot that in the late seventeenth century a "dissociation of sensibility" had set in. He later described his own enterprise as to lay the ghost of Descartes. Literature as thought, for example in the best work of Lawrence, was able to grant us a sense of wholeness by which to live. One of Leavis's favorite quotations from Lawrence was that Lawrence wrote out of his moral and religious sense, "For the race, as it were."[1] The enlightenment and the industrial revolution had broken continuity. While Leavis agreed with Lawrence that the whole of modern civilization was collapsing, he nevertheless felt that the fresh shoots of life, which Lawrence believed must be nurtured, could only be so by remembering the tradition that had been lost. Leavis's whole work as a literary critic was to discriminate the best works of literature that could sustain culture and provide for a truly human future. Throughout, he believed that the minority capable of making such judgments must be allowed to do its work, whether within an English school that formed the vital center of a university or in the pages of a critical review like *Scrutiny* or *The Human World* that could equally provide such a center. In Leavis's view, great literature ("the best that has been thought and said") asked the important questions about human living: What for? What ultimately for? What do human beings live by?

At a time when English departments are hurrying to make themselves over into departments of cultural studies in which studying sports magazines will be thought as important as reading *King Lear,* Leavis offers a salutary reminder. Only by studying the best writing can the best ideas be generated. Our culture will not be saved by reading, even critically analyzing or theorizing about sports magazines. Studying great literature can, however, at least make us aware of the best that has been thought and said. Such was certainly the belief, fully lived out, of the greatest English literary critic of the twentieth century—F. R. Leavis. Though he lacked formal religion, he had a religious sense of the importance to human culture of a vital literary tradition. Though Wordsworth and Eliot were major poets who "altered expression" in their time, Shakespeare, Blake, Dickens, and Lawrence were the literary geniuses who had carried through a vital tradition in English language and thought that constituted a great and living literature.

Notes and References

Chapter One

1. Biographical details are taken from Ian Robinson, "F. R. Leavis The Cambridge Don," for University College, Swansea English Society, 17 March 1992, hereafter cited in text as Robinson 1992; Ian MacKillop, *F. R. Leavis: A Life in Criticism* (London: Allen Lane-Penguin, 1995), hereafter cited in text; Ian MacKillop and Richard Storer, eds., *F. R. Leavis: Essays and Documents* (Sheffield, U.K.: Sheffield Academic Press, 1995), hereafter cited in text; and G. S. Singh, *F. R. Leavis: A Literary Biography with Q. D. Leavis's "Memoir" of F. R. Leavis* (London: Duckworth, 1995), hereafter cited in text.

2. The house and garden are described in loving detail by Q. D. Leavis in her "Memoir" included in Singh, 23–25.

3. MacKillop cites the Cambridge County Record Office.

4. Mary Pitter, "6, Chesterton Hall Crescent, and the early years" in *The Leavises: Recollections and Impressions,* ed. Denys Thompson (Cambridge: Cambridge University Press, 1984), 21; Thompson hereafter cited in text.

5. Reprinted with a "Note: Leavis at school" in Thompson, 184–86.

6. F. R. Leavis, "Wordsworth: The Creative Conditions," in *The Critic As Anti-Philosopher,* ed. G. S. Singh (London: Chatto and Windus, 1982), 37; hereafter cited in text as "Wordsworth."

7. From Student's Handbook (1919), pp. 404–5. Cited by MacKillop, 56.

8. F. R. Leavis, Introduction to *John Stuart Mill on Bentham and Coleridge* (New York: Harper and Row, 1962), 3.

9. F. R. Leavis, "Two Cultures? The Significance of Lord Snow" in *Nor Shall My Sword: Discourses on Pluralism, Compassion, and Social Hope* (London: Chatto and Windus, 1972), 62; hereafter cited in text as "TC."

10. MacKillop, 350–60; and see responses to MacKillop's biography in the *Cambridge Quarterly* 25, no. 4 (1996) for further comments on this controversy.

11. It was first published in the United States in 1971.

12. "The Third Realm: Ten Years' Work by F. R. Leavis," *The Human World* 3 (May 1971): 71; hereafter cited in text as "Third Realm."

13. F. R. Leavis, *Two Cultures? The Significance of C. P. Snow* (London: Chatto and Windus, 1962), 27–28.

Chapter Two

1. Q. D. Leavis, "Professor Chadwick and English Studies (1947)" in *A Selection from Scrutiny*. Compiled by F. R. Leavis (Cambridge: Cambridge University Press, 1968), 1:45.

2. F. R. Leavis, "The Relationship of Journalism to Literature: Studied in the Rise and Earlier Development of the Press in England" (Ph.D. diss., Cambridge University, 1924), 7; hereafter cited in text as "RJ."

3. F. R. Leavis, *Mass Civilisation and Minority Culture* (Cambridge: Minority Press, 1930), 16; hereafter cited in text as *MCMC*.

4. F. R. Leavis, *D. H. Lawrence* (Cambridge: Minority Press, 1930); hereafter cited in text as *DHL*.

5. F. R. Leavis, *New Bearings in English Poetry: A Study of the Contemporary Situation* (Cambridge: Minority Press, 1930), 19; hereafter cited in text as *NBEP.*

Chapter Three

1. F. R. Leavis, *How to Teach Reading: A Primer for Ezra Pound,* appendix to *Education and the University: A Sketch for an "English School,"* by F. R. Leavis (London: Chatto and Windus, 1943), 105; hereafter cited in text as *HTTR*.

2. F. R. Leavis, "Introduction," in *Towards Standards of Criticism: Selections from "The Calendar of Modern Letters, 1925–1927,"* ed. F. R. Leavis (London: Wishart, 1933), 9; hereafter cited in text as *TSOC*.

3. F. R. Leavis, *For Continuity* (Cambridge: Minority Press, 1933); hereafter cited in text as *FC*.

4. F. R. Leavis and Denys Thompson, *Culture and Environment: The Training of Critical Awareness* (London: Chatto and Windus, 1933), 1–2; hereafter cited in text as *CE*.

5. F. R. Leavis, ed. *Determinations: Critical Essays.* With an Introduction by F. R. Leavis. (1934; reprint, New York: Haskell House, 1970), 2.

6. F. R. Leavis, *Revaluation: Tradition and Development in English Poetry* (London: Chatto and Windus, 1936), 9; hereafter cited in text as *R*.

7. See "Appendix: Notes on Wordsworth" in F. R. Leavis, *Valuation in Criticism and Other Essays,* ed. G. S. Singh (Cambridge: Cambridge University Press, 1986), 299; hereafter cited in text as "Notes."

Chapter Four

1. The exception is G. D. Klingopoulos's essay "The Novel as Dramatic Poem (II): 'Wuthering Heights,' " *Scrutiny* 14, no. 4 (September 1947): 269–86. Otherwise the series begun in *Scrutiny* in Spring 1947 contained Leavis's essays on: (I) *Hard Times, Scrutiny* 14, no. 3 (Spring 1947): 185–203; (III) *The Europeans, Scrutiny* 15, no. 3 (Summer 1948): 209–21; (IV) *St. Mawr, Scrutiny* 17, no. 1 (Spring 1950): 38–53; (V) *Women in Love* (1) *Scrutiny* 17, no.

3 (Autumn 1950): 203–20, (2) *Scrutiny* 17, no. 4 (March 1951): 318–30, (3) *Scrutiny* 18, no. 1 (June 1951): 18–31; (VI) *The Rainbow* (1) *Scrutiny* 18, no. 3 (Winter 1951–1952): 197–210, (2) *Scrutiny* 18, no. 4 (June 1952): 273–87, (3) *Scrutiny* 19, no. 1 (October 1952): 15–30.

    2. F. R. Leavis, "Dickens and Blake: *Little Dorrit,*" in *Dickens the Novelist,* by F. R. Leavis and Q. D. Leavis (London: Chatto and Windus, 1970), 213–76; hereafter cited in text as *DN*.

    3. F. R. Leavis, "The Americanness of American Literature" in *"Anna Karenina" and Other Essays* (London: Chatto and Windus, 1967), 145–46.

    4. F. R. Leavis, "The Teaching of Literature (3): The Literary Discipline and Liberal Education," *Sewanee Review* 55 (1947) 586–609.

    5. M. B. Kinch, William Baker, and John Kimber, *F. R. Leavis and Q. D. Leavis: An Annotated Bibliography* (New York: Garland, 1969), section M 170, 209.

    6. R. P. Bilan, "The Basic Concepts and Criteria of F. R. Leavis's Novel Criticism," *Novel* 9, no. 3 (Spring 1976): 197–216.

    7. F. R. Leavis, "*Hard Times:* An Analytic Note," in *The Great Tradition: George Eliot, Henry James, and Joseph Conrad* (1948; reprint, London: Penguin, 1962), 249; hereafter cited in text as *GT.*

    8. F. R. Leavis, "*The Europeans,*" in *"Anna Karenina" and Other Essays* (London: Chatto and Windus, 1967), 59; hereafter cited in text as *"E."*

    9. All of these that were published between 1957 and 1967, with the exception of *Dombey and Son,* which appears in *Dickens the Novelist* (1970), are reprinted in *"Anna Karenina" and Other Essays* (London: Chatto and Windus, 1967).

Chapter Five

    1. T. S. Eliot, *Four Quartets* (1944; London: Faber and Faber, 1958), 23; hereafter cited in text as *Four Quartets.*

    2. C. P. Snow, *The Two Cultures: And a Second Look* (Cambridge: Cambridge University Press, 1964), 22; hereafter cited in text.

    3. F. R. Leavis, "Luddites? or There is Only One Culture," in *Nor Shall My Sword: Discourses on Pluralism, Compassion, and Social Hope* (London: Chatto and Windus, 1972), 77; hereafter cited in text as "Luddites."

    4. F. R. Leavis, "'English,' Unrest, and Continuity," in *Nor Shall My Sword: Discourses on Pluralism, Compassion, and Social Hope* (London: Chatto and Windus, 1972), 104; hereafter cited in text as "English."

    5. F. R. Leavis, "Pluralism, Compassion, and Social Hope," in *Nor Shall My Sword: Discourses on Pluralism, Compassion, and Social Hope* (London: Chatto and Windus, 1972), 171; hereafter cited in text as "Pluralism."

    6. F. R. Leavis, "'Literarism' versus 'Scientism': the Misconception and the Menace," in *Nor Shall My Sword: Discourses on Pluralism, Compassion, and Social Hope* (London: Chatto and Windus, 1972), 151; hereafter cited in text as "Literarism."

7. F. R. Leavis, "Élites, Oligarchies, and an Educated Public," in *Nor Shall My Sword: Discourses on Pluralism, Compassion, and Social Hope* (London: Chatto and Windus, 1972), 207; hereafter cited in text as "Elites."

Chapter Six

1. F. R. Leavis, *The Living Principle: "English" As a Discipline of Thought* (London: Chatto and Windus, 1975), 13; hereafter cited in text as *LP.*
2. Ian Robinson, *The Survival of English: Essays in Criticism of Language* (Cambridge: Cambridge University Press, 1973), 239.
3. D. H. Lawrence, quoted in F. R. Leavis, *Thought, Words, and Creativity: Art and Thought in Lawrence* (London: Chatto and Windus, 1976), 7; hereafter cited in text as *TWC.*
4. F. R. Leavis, "Introductory: 'Life *Is* a Necessary Word,'" in *Nor Shall My Sword: Discourses on Pluralism, Compassion, and Social Hope* (London: Chatto and Windus, 1972), 9–37.

Chapter Seven

1. F. R. Leavis, "Thought, Meaning, and Sensibility: The Problem of Value Judgment," in *Valuation in Criticism and Other Essays,* ed. G. S. Singh (Cambridge: Cambridge University Press, 1986), 297.

Selected Bibliography

Within each section of the Bibliography items appear chronologically according to the date of publication.

PRIMARY WORKS

"The Relationship of Journalism to Literature: Studied in the Rise and Earlier Development of the Press in England." Ph.D. diss., Cambridge University, 1924.

D. H. Lawrence. Cambridge: Minority Press, 1930.

Mass Civilisation and Minority Culture. Cambridge: Minority Press, 1930.

How to Teach Reading: A Primer for Ezra Pound. Cambridge: Minority Press, 1932.

New Bearings in English Poetry: A Study of the Contemporary Situation. London: Chatto and Windus, 1932.

F. R. Leavis and Denys Thompson. *Culture and Environment: The Training of Critical Awareness.* London: Chatto and Windus, 1933.

For Continuity. Cambridge: Minority Press, 1933.

Towards Standards of Criticism: Selections from "The Calendar of Modern Letters, 1925–1927." Chosen with an introduction by F. R. Leavis. London: Wishart, 1933.

Determinations: Critical Essays. London: Chatto and Windus, 1934.

Revaluation: Tradition and Development in English Poetry. London: Chatto and Windus, 1936.

Education and the University: A Sketch for an "English School." London: Chatto and Windus, 1943.

The Great Tradition: George Eliot, Henry James, and Joseph Conrad. London: Chatto and Windus, 1948.

Mill on Bentham and Coleridge. Introduction by F. R. Leavis. London: Chatto and Windus, 1950.

The Common Pursuit. London: Chatto and Windus, 1952.

D. H. Lawrence: Novelist. London: Chatto and Windus, 1955.

Two Cultures? The Significance of C. P. Snow. With an essay by Michael Yudkin. London: Chatto and Windus, 1962.

"*Scrutiny:* A Retrospect. " In Volume 20 of *Scrutiny.* Reissued ed. Cambridge: Cambridge University Press, 1963.

"Anna Karenina" and Other Essays. London: Chatto and Windus, 1967.

English Literature in Our Time and the University: Clark Lectures 1967. London: Chatto and Windus, 1969.

F. R. Leavis and Q. D. Leavis. *Lectures in America.* London: Chatto and Windus, 1969.

F. R. Leavis and Q. D. Leavis. *Dickens the Novelist.* London: Chatto and Windus, 1970.

Nor Shall My Sword: Discourses on Pluralism, Compassion, and Social Hope. London: Chatto and Windus, 1972.

Letters in Criticism. Ed. John Tasker. London: Chatto and Windus, 1974.

The Living Principle: "English" As a Discipline of Thought. London: Chatto and Windus, 1975.

Thought, Words, and Creativity: Art and Thought in Lawrence. London: Chatto and Windus, 1976.

The Critic As Anti-Philosopher: Essays and Papers. Ed. G. S. Singh. London: Chatto and Windus, 1982.

Valuation in Criticism and Other Essays. Ed. G. S. Singh. Cambridge: Cambridge University Press, 1986.

More Letters in Criticism by F. R. Leavis and Q. D. Leavis. Ed. M. B. Kinch. Bradford on Avon: privately printed, 1992.

Bibliography

Kinch, M. B., William Baker, and John Kimber. *F. R. Leavis and Q. D. Leavis: An Annotated Bibliography.* New York and London: Garland, 1989. According to Kinch, Baker, and Kimber, this is "the first fully annotated bibliography of writings by and about two of the most important and controversial literary critics of the 20th century."

SECONDARY WORKS

Buckley, Vincent. *Poetry and Morality: Studies on the Criticism of Matthew Arnold, T. S. Eliot, and F. R. Leavis.* London: Chatto and Windus, 1968. An early study of Leavis as a moral critic.

Hayman, Ronald. *Leavis.* London: Heinemann, 1976. The first full-length study.

Watson, Garry. *The Leavises, the "Social," and the Left.* Swansea, U.K.: Brynmill Press, 1977. An important study of the Leavises' treatment by the London literary and left-wing establishments.

Boyers, Robert. *F. R. Leavis: Judgment and the Discipline of Thought.* Columbia: University of Missouri Press, 1978. The first North American study.

Greenwood, Edward. *F. R. Leavis.* Harlow, U.K.: Longman, 1978. A useful pamphlet in the Writers and Their Work series.

Bilan, R. P. *The Literary Criticism of F. R. Leavis.* Cambridge: Cambridge University Press, 1979. The first detailed, full-length study issuing from a doctoral thesis.

Mulhern, Francis. *The Moment of "Scrutiny."* London: New Left Books, 1979. A study of *Scrutiny* from a Marxist perspective.

French, Philip. *Three Honest Men: Edmund Wilson, F. R. Leavis, Lionel Trilling.* Manchester, U.K.: Carcanet Press, 1980. An 80th birthday tribute prepared for the BBC Third Programme.

Walsh, William. *F. R. Leavis.* London: Chatto and Windus, 1980. An appreciative study.

Robertson, P. J. M. *The Leavises on Fiction: An Historic Partnership.* London: Macmillan, 1981. A helpful study of the Leavises on the novel.

Strickland, Geoffrey. "The Criticism of F. R. Leavis." In *Structuralism or Criticism? Thoughts on How We Read.* Cambridge: Cambridge University Press, 1981. Leavis's criticism contrasted with Roland Barthes's utopianism.

McCallum, Pamela. *Literature and Method: Towards a Critique of I. A. Richards, T. S. Eliot, and F. R. Leavis.* Dublin: Gill and Macmillan, 1983. "The polarisation of society and consciousness" in Leavis's criticism.

Thompson, Denys, ed. *The Leavises: Recollections and Impressions.* Cambridge: Cambridge University Press, 1984. Reminiscences by people who knew the Leavises.

Bell, Michael. *F. R. Leavis.* London: Routledge, 1988. Considers Leavis in relation to European philosophy.

Bergonzi, Bernard. "Leavis, Lewis, and Other Oppositions." In *Exploding English: Criticism, Theory, Culture.* Oxford: Clarendon Press, 1990. Leavis's and C. S. Lewis's differing approaches to English Studies.

Samson, Anne. *F. R. Leavis.* Toronto: University of Toronto Press, 1992. Leavis considered in a series on modern cultural theorists.

MacKillop, Ian. *F. R. Leavis: A Life in Criticism.* London: Allen Lane-Penguin, 1995. A detailed biographical study.

MacKillop, Ian, and Richard Storer, eds. *F. R. Leavis: Essays and Documents.* Sheffield, U.K.: Academic Press, 1995. Bibliographical, educational, analytical and biographical essays on Leavis.

Singh, G. S. *F. R. Leavis: A Literary Biography with Q. D. Leavis's "Memoir" of F. R. Leavis.* London: Duckworth, 1995. A biographical study by one of the Leavises' literary executors that includes Q. D. Leavis's "Memoir" of her husband.

Day, Gary. *Re-Reading Leavis: Culture and Literary Criticism.* London: Macmillan, 1996. A re-reading of Leavis by a critical and cultural theorist.

Index

127

The Author

John Ferns was born in 1941 in Ottawa, Ontario. He was educated at King Edward VI's School, Birmingham, and St. Edmund Hall, Oxford, where he received an Honors B.A. He received a Diploma of Education from the University of Nottingham and an M.A. and Ph.D. from the University of Western Ontario, where he held a Commonwealth Scholarship, a Canada Council Pre-Doctoral Fellowship, and a Queen Elizabeth II Scholarship.

Since 1970, Professor Ferns has been a member of the faculty of Humanities at McMaster University, Hamilton, Ontario, where he now holds the position of professor of English. During 1976–1977 he held a Leave Fellowship from the Canada Council while on sabbatical leave at the Centre of Canadian Studies, University of Edinburgh, Scotland. From 1985 to 1986 he was a visiting research fellow in the Department of English and Comparative Literary Studies at the University of Warwick, England, while holding a Leave Fellowship from the Social Sciences and Humanities Research Council of Canada. From 1982 to 1985 he was associate dean of Humanities (Studies) and from 1994 to 1997 chair of the M.A.(T)-M.Sc.(T) Programme at McMaster. He has published two earlier studies in Twayne's World Authors and English Authors Series, on Canadian poet, critic, and anthologist A. J. M. Smith (1979) and on English biographer and critic Lytton Strachey (1988). He is the author of five volumes of poetry: *The Antlered Boy* (1970), *Henry Hudson* (1975), *The Snow Horses* (1977), *From The River* (1985), and *Affirmations* (1989). With Brian Crick he is co-editor of George Whalley's *Studies in Literature and the Humanities: Innocence of Intent* (1985) and with Kevin McCabe of *The Poetry of Lucy Maud Montgomery* (1987). He is a deacon at St. George's Reformed Episcopal Church, Hamilton, Ontario.

The Editor

Kinley E. Roby is professor emeritus of English at Northeastern University. He is the twentieth-century field editor of Twayne's English Authors Series, series editor of Twayne's Critical History of British Drama, and general editor of Twayne's Women and Literature Series. He has written books on Arnold Bennett, Edward VII, and Joyce Cary and has edited a collection of essays on T. S. Eliot. He makes his home in Naples, Florida.

R

AOX-9532

WITHDRAWN